VAT Registration

Unravelling the Complexities
2nd edition

Graham Elliott

© **Claritax Books Ltd (February 2018)**

All rights reserved. No part of this publication may be reproduced or distributed in any form or by any means, or stored in a database or retrieval system, without the prior written permission of the publishers.

Official material is reproduced under the terms of the Open Government Licence (see www.nationalarchives.gov.uk/doc/open-government-licence).

Disclaimer

This publication is sold with the understanding that neither the publishers nor the authors, with regard to this publication, are engaged in providing legal or professional services.

The material contained in this publication does not constitute tax advice and readers are advised that they should always obtain such professional advice before acting, or refraining from acting, on any information contained in this book. Readers are also advised that UK tax law is subject to frequent and unpredictable change.

Every effort has been taken to compile the contents of this book accurately and carefully. However, neither the publisher nor the author can accept any responsibility or liability to any person, whether a purchaser of this book or not, in respect of anything done or omitted to be done by any such person in reliance, partly or wholly, on any part or on the whole of the contents of this book.

First edition (VAT Registration Handbook) April 2014
This edition February 2018

VAT Registration

Unravelling the Complexities
2nd edition

Graham Elliott

Published by:

Claritax Books Ltd
6 Grosvenor Park Road
Chester, CH1 1QQ

www.claritaxbooks.com

ISBN: 978-1-912386-00-0

Other titles from Claritax Books

Other titles from Claritax Books include:

- A-Z of Plant & Machinery
- Advising British Expats
- Capital Allowances
- Construction Industry Scheme
- Discovery Assessments
- Employee Benefits & Expenses
- Employment Status
- Entrepreneurs' Relief
- Financial Planning with Trusts
- Furnished Holiday Lettings
- Main Residence Relief
- Pension Tax Guide
- Research & Development
- Residence: The Definition in Practice
- Stamp Duty Land Tax
- Tax Chamber Hearings
- Tax Losses
- Venture Capital Schemes

See www.claritaxbooks.com for further details of all the above books (including extracts and full tables of contents), and for information about further titles due for publication in the coming months.

About the author

Graham Elliott is the director of City & Cambridge Consultancy, which provides VAT advice to owner managed businesses, charities, private individuals, and professional advisers. He has practised as a VAT Consultant for 30 years, and has been involved in VAT in wider capacities for around 35 years. Over the last fifteen or so years his range has broadened somewhat, but his work is still predominantly in the VAT sphere.

Graham is a Chartered Tax Adviser and an MBA (from Warwick University). He sees the combination of tax technical knowledge and an understanding of how business works as being key to his ability to provide relevant and insightful advice to his clients.

In 2011 he won "Tax Writer of the Year" in the LexisNexis Taxation Awards. In his citation the judges commented that he is "a writer who does not just accept the status quo, and who manages to make VAT interesting". His approach to writing and talking about the subject, whether in the course of advising clients or more generally, is based on that ethos, and on the principle that a persuasive and memorable account of the issues is more likely to provide value to the recipient and ensure that actions are taken.

Graham has spent most of his advisory career in accountancy practices, mainly at senior levels.

Graham can be emailed at graham@cityandcambridgeconsultancy.com and has a profile on Linkedin at www.linkedin.com/in/grahampelliott.

About the publisher

Claritax Books publishes specialist tax titles, complementing what is on offer from the larger tax publishers. Typically, our books cover niche topics in greater depth or take a more practical approach to particular tax issues. Our titles are written for accountants (both in-house and in practice), tax advisers, employers, lawyers and other professionals. Our authors include barristers, solicitors, accountants and other experienced tax specialists.

Claritax Books titles cover (among other topics) tax appeals, capital allowances, the statutory residence rules, CGT reliefs, the CIS scheme, pensions and trusts, stamp duty land tax, VAT, employment taxes and furnished holiday lettings. Visit www.claritaxbooks.com for details of all our books.

Claritax Books is a trading name of Claritax Books Ltd (company number 07658388, VAT number 114 9371 20). The company is based in Chester, England.

Abbreviations

B2B	Business-to-business
B2C	Business-to-customer
Ch.	Chapter
CEC	Commission of the European Communities
CJEU	Court of Justice of the European Union
EAT	Employment Appeal Tribunal
EU	European Union
EWCA	England and Wales Court of Appeal
EWHC	High Court of England and Wales
FA	Finance Act
HMRC	Her Majesty's Revenue & Customs
MOSS	Mini One Stop Shop
NI	National Insurance
OTS	Office of Tax Simplification
Para.	Paragraph
Pt.	Part
Reg.	Regulation
S.	Section
Sch.	Schedule
SDLT	Stamp duty land tax
SI	Statutory Instrument
TC	Tax Chamber
TOGC	Transfer of Going Concern
TOMS	Tour Operators Margin Scheme
UKFTT	UK First-tier Tribunal
UKSC	UK Supreme Court
UKUT	UK Upper Tribunal
VAT	Value Added Tax
VATA 1994	Value Added Tax Act 1994
VATPOSS	VAT Place of Supply of Services Manual
VGROUPS	VAT Groups Manual

Foreword

This is the second edition of this book, which I originally managed to write with considerable assistance from one or two fellow professionals and my then firm. But for the last three years or so I have run my own practice, nevertheless retaining my clients, and adding some new ones, and this allows me to determine what I can and cannot do. This naturally reduces the scope of the thanks I need to offer. However, I wish to thank Claritax Books for believing in the book sufficiently to go to the considerable effort of issuing a second edition. I would also like to pay tribute to my clients for the support they have provided along the way, and the provision of examples of relevant issues which are discussed in this book.

Graham Elliott

February 2018

Table of contents

Other titles from Claritax Books iv
About the author v
About the publisher vii
Abbreviations viii
Foreword ix
Introduction 1

1. Pros and cons of registration
    1.1   Introduction 3
    1.2   Risk mitigation 3
    1.3   Fiscal advantage 5
    1.4   General commercial advantages 6
    1.5   The obvious disadvantage 7
    1.6   Summary 7

2. Compulsory registration criteria
    2.1   Introduction 8
    2.2   Who or what must register? 8
    2.3   Taxable supplies criteria 9
    2.4   Transfer of a going concern 20
    2.5   Further grounds for registration arising from
           international activity 28

3. Defining "supplies"
    3.1   Situations regarded as supplies 41
    3.2   Barter 41
    3.3   Face value vouchers 42
    3.4   Imported services 43
    3.5   Self supplies 46
    3.6   Supply valuation 48

4. Cases where supplies can appear to be hidden
    4.1   Introduction 49
    4.2   Supply of staff 49
    4.3   Compensation 51
    4.4   Management services 54

	4.5	Phoney management services 55
	4.6	Delayed consideration between related companies 56
	4.7	Intercompany debts 57
	4.8	Disbursements 59
	4.9	Hotels 61

5. Whether a business
	5.1	"Business" and "economic activity" 62
	5.2	Recognising a business 63
	5.3	Illegal activity 79

6. Agent or principal?
	6.1	Introduction 80
	6.2	Case law 81
	6.3	Agent acting as principal 86
	6.4	Tour operators 87

7. Profit or consideration?
	7.1	Joint business activity 88
	7.2	Land 89

8. Business fragmentation
	8.1	HMRC defences 92
	8.2	Directions to be treated as one entity 92
	8.3	Retrospective application 97
	8.4	General observations 99

9. Voluntary registration
	9.1	Reasons to register voluntarily 101
	9.2	Land and property 102
	9.3	Proving intention to trade 103
	9.4	Speculative ventures 104
	9.5	Nature of taxable supplies for purposes of voluntary registration 104
	9.6	Voluntary registration for acquisitions from other EU states 105
	9.7	Voluntary registration for distance selling 105

10. "Waiver" of registration
- 10.1 Introduction 107
- 10.2 Zero-rated supplies 107
- 10.3 Turnover 108

11. Groups of companies
- 11.1 The purposes of group registration 109
- 11.2 Who joins? 110
- 11.3 Entity criteria 111
- 11.4 Control criteria 112
- 11.5 Specific HMRC powers 118
- 11.6 Further anti-avoidance provisions 120
- 11.7 Timing of the application 121
- 11.8 Phantom groups 124
- 11.9 Leaving the group 124

12. Divisional registration 126

13. De-registering from VAT
- 13.1 Introduction 127
- 13.2 Voluntary de-registration 127
- 13.3 Compulsory de-registration 130
- 13.4 Disadvantages of de-registering 132

14. Penalties
- 14.1 Introduction 133
- 14.2 Honest error 133
- 14.3 Dishonest error 134
- 14.4 Pre April 2010 penalties 135
- 14.5 Reasonable excuse case 135
- 14.6 Security payment 136

15. Completing the forms
- 15.1 Introduction 137
- 15.2 Applicable forms 137
- 15.3 Information with application 138
- 15.4 Partnership application 139
- 15.5 Group application 139
- 15.6 Isle of Man 140
- 15.7 Transferring the old VAT number 141

16. The flat rate scheme
- 16.1 Introduction 142
- 16.2 The purpose of the scheme 142
- 16.3 Qualification for joining..143
- 16.4 Qualification for remaining in the scheme 144
- 16.5 Other causes of either leaving the scheme or not qualifying for it *ab initio*..145
- 16.6 Issues arising from accounting under the scheme.......146
- 16.7 Scheme percentages and the first-year discount..........147
- 16.8 Flat rate for low cost traders from April 2017..............148
- 16.9 Conclusion..149

17. Policy issues relating to registration 150

Appendix – Historic VAT registration thresholds 155

Table of primary legislation 157
Table of secondary legislation 159
Index of cases...161
General index...163

Introduction

Why write a book purely about VAT registration? To put it another way, a question put to me by one of my fellow VAT advisers was, is there really enough in VAT registration as a stand-alone subject for a book?

The justification for a single volume dealing with VAT registration can be made from at least two perspectives. First, the subject is larger than it may initially seem. HMRC's highly comprehensive manuals of guidance for their own officers is considerably longer than this book. This compendious resource (available on the HMRC website) covers a range of things that are not necessarily and exclusively to do with registration, but it does illustrate a number of situations that need to be considered in association with VAT registration.

The second reason is that for many practitioners at whom this book is aimed, often accountants and business advisers, the first thing they have to do for their clients, in relation to VAT, is register them or decide that registration is not needed. It is, so to speak, the first critical interface in any contentious or potentially difficult situation arising from VAT and, as the first chapter of this book aims to illustrate, it can be a very contentious and difficult area indeed if things do not go to plan.

On a purely physical level, the existence of a separate book on the bookshelf serves as a reminder that this is a subject that needs to be addressed both at the inception of any new business, and at any point in time prior to a business actually being registered. Otherwise, with the best will in the world, handling the VAT registration obligations can too easily be overlooked. Indeed, I am sure we have all been faced with situations where we have enquired about the VAT treatment of a set of circumstances, only to be met by the comment that "there is no VAT because we are not VAT registered". That ought immediately to beg the question: "Why not?" Too often it is met with a welcoming shrug of the shoulders. Everybody assumes that it must be right without further question. But what is needed, above all things, is a sceptical mind.

Introduction

This book attempts to draw together all of the circumstances in which VAT registration might be a requirement, might be desirable, or might require more than one entity to be recognised and registered as such. It deals with the possibilities of grouping more than one company together in a registration, with de-registration, and with many other aspects besides. In doing so, it covers a number of more general but relevant points, such as what constitutes consideration, what constitutes a business, whether our activity is as an agent or principal, whether two or more ostensibly separate businesses are really one business, and whether we have moved into the realms of "barter". All of these have a direct bearing on the issue of registration and de-registration.

The book is restricted to the UK VAT rules, and whilst a nodding acquaintance is made with the overarching EU law principles, the text does not cover VAT registration in any other EU member state, or elsewhere in the world. That said, the book provides food for thought in regard to other jurisdictions. There will, indeed, be some rules which have a direct parallel in other EU states, and which are derived from EU principles which apply absolutely equally across the entire Union.

Although most of the book is given over to points of practice which are to do with technical and theoretical matters, the practical considerations of "filling in the forms" have not been ignored. The difficulty here, though, is that the forms can change rapidly, and HMRC can amend the format quite frequently. It would therefore limit this book's shelf life if it was too prescriptive over the purely administrative matters. Comments have been made as regards the position at the time of writing, but with the caveat that the reader will need to refer to HMRC's own literature (which is, one hopes, constantly being developed) to determine the specific actions that have to be taken to effect a registration or de-registration.

And thus, the main overarching aim of this book is to try to keep people out of trouble. It deals with advantages and disadvantages along the way.

The text is based on the law as at 1 February 2018.

1. Pros and cons of registration

1.1 Introduction

The title of this chapter may appear alarming, since most people associate VAT registration with an obligation rather than as something that could give an advantage. But there are two ways in which applying for VAT registration could be regarded as giving some kind of advantage:

- reducing risk; and
- obtaining a better fiscal outcome.[1]

1.2 Risk mitigation

1.2.1 Nature of the risks

As will become clear in a later chapter, VAT registration rules set specific deadlines by which to apply, failing which there is a risk of penalties. In general, however, it is possible to apply for VAT registration sooner rather than later. Accordingly, being registered on what may appear to be the early side of what is required constitutes a risk mitigation strategy.

It is often forgotten that the normal time limitation on HMRC for assessment (generally four years) only applies to an entity which is already registered for VAT. By contrast, where an entity is not registered for VAT, the time limitation extends to twenty years (VATA 1994, s. 77(4)). This in turn gives rise to the following risks:

1. The amount of the VAT applicable to supplies made over the full 20-year period (or even a substantial proportion of it) would be a figure that could easily bankrupt a business, and is particularly dangerous where the business format does not give rise to limited liability for the people who have operated the business (such as with sole proprietorships and traditional partnerships).

---

[1] By "fiscal" I mean a financially improved position deriving from tax, as distinct from an administrative advantage.

Pros and cons of registration

2. Over such a long period it is unlikely that it will be possible to amass sufficient evidence of VAT-bearing expenditure to offset a sufficient amount of input tax recovery against the sales made, such as to reduce the liability to what it would have been had the business been registered at the right time. (It should be noted, however, that HMRC have powers to estimate a more realistic input tax deduction, but it seems at least probable that that would undershoot what might have been available.)

3. A person may have decided to run the business on the basis that it was making a profit without having considered that, if accounting for VAT on that business, it would not have been making a profit. Had the business been registered for VAT at the right time, this might have led to a change of business model, to a decision to shut the business, or to diversification in order to create profit. What this means is that the business was prolonged beyond its useful life, or run in an unsatisfactory manner, under the illusion of making a profit. It is particularly unfortunate in a case where a person had decided to be an entrepreneur rather than an employee, but could have made considerably more money as an employee without the attendant VAT risks.

4. There may have been some opportunity within the business model to charge VAT to parties that could reclaim it, but this would have been missed entirely unless either the records were exceptionally good, and thus former customers can be traced, and any of those customers have the ability to claim the VAT charged to them.

1.2.2 A sad example

The saddest example of this happening, in the author's experience, relates to the first-tier tribunal decision in the case of *Susan Evans*.

Mrs Evans had operated a retail unit which was of marginal profitability, even leaving aside her failure to register for VAT. While some of her products were zero-rated, a number were standard rated. Neither she nor her accountant had spotted the possibility that she needed to register for VAT. At a very late stage (some ten years in) HMRC cross referred to her self assessment returns, and made an enquiry. She was found to be registerable for a number of years. The liability was finally settled at around £10,000. For her this was an enormous sum.

The case came forward on the basis of whether she should suffer a penalty on top of this, but clearly the tax alone was a crippling figure for a lady who was by that time in her seventies, and had almost nothing to live on by way of a pension, having had a less than lucrative commercial career. Whilst the tribunal decision could not, of course, go into the question of "what might have been" had she registered for VAT on time, there seems little doubt that she would have noticed that her small profits were in reality losses, and would have shut the business before she had accrued more liabilities. She might have sought employment, or a different business model, elsewhere. As it happened, however, it was not possible to rewrite history, and thus she owed the VAT (though thankfully the tribunal decided to strike out the penalties).

Furthermore, it was simply not possible for the tribunal to apply any concept of "reasonable excuse", or compassionate grounds, to reduce the actual tax liability itself, despite the fact that the taxpayer may well not have incurred that level of tax had she been aware of the position at an early date.

This extremely sad case is a salutary lesson concerning the perils of not being registered for VAT.

Case: *Susan Evans v HMRC* [2011] UKFTT 464 (TC)

1.3 Fiscal advantage

There are three basic sources of fiscal advantage which ought to be considered when weighing up the pros and cons of VAT registration:

1. That the customer, if it is a business which is making taxable supplies, can reclaim all or the majority of the VAT which may be added to the price, thus leaving the business in a position to reclaim input tax without a corresponding erosion of its revenue stream (all of which has to be checked with each customer).

2. All or the majority of the supplies made by the business may be zero-rated (such as sales of printed material, certain kinds of food, new housing etc.) which will allow VAT to be claimed from HMRC, but with no corresponding output tax. This could even apply where the supplies are reduced rated and thus the input tax is greater than the output tax for that reason.
3. The business is structurally loss-making (such as is not uncommon with a charity) so that the VAT-bearing costs are higher than the VAT bearing income.

Clearly, these benefits have to be weighed up carefully, since not all businesses can reclaim VAT, and supplies that are zero-rated might revert to being subject to a positive rate of VAT in the future, or the business may change its products. However, given that this cannot really be avoided because, in most cases, the registration will be compulsory, this is not of itself a particular concern. Where registration is voluntary (on which more later) it may be possible to de-register from VAT voluntarily if the position becomes adverse.

It is also conceivable that an advantage will arise from the deployment of the partial exemption *de minimis* limits which will allow full VAT recovery even though a certain amount of exempt activity is undertaken, but this is a highly technical area which is beyond the scope of this book.

1.4 General commercial advantages

Although deciding to register for VAT on a voluntary basis is not normally based on a purely commercial advantage, it is obvious that the fact that a business making taxable supplies on a certain scale must, by law, be registered for VAT, gives rise to a perception that a VAT registered business has such scale. A customer will not know, for instance, that the business is voluntarily registered for VAT at an embryonic stage if it receives a VAT invoice. This therefore gives the impression of a more established business. It also wards off fears that the business has deliberately failed to account for VAT which is due, and even though this may well not be the case, that concern is allayed by actually charging VAT. It is not impossible that certain potential customers would be unable to enter into a contract with a non-VAT registered company on the basis that it does not pass this rough and ready compliance test. It is likely that this kind of self-policed compliance approach will become more marked over time, thus giving small businesses an incentive for registering for VAT.

1.5 The obvious disadvantage

Obviously there is a disadvantage to registering for VAT when one might not have to have done so. This is generally that VAT will be imposed on an income stream without the ability of the customer to reclaim it (particularly in B2C sales, or where the business contracts heavily with exempt service providers such as those in finance, housing, education, and care). In that case the input tax will generally be a lower value than the output tax, so a net loss has to be accepted by the business, or its charges become effectively uncompetitive.

1.6 Summary

Whilst the title of this section may appear strange, in suggesting that it is better to be registered for VAT than not, there are good reasons, particularly on the compliance side of the equation, to become registered.

From the standpoint of the professional adviser, registering clients promptly for VAT removes another item from the "to-do list" which could otherwise be overlooked with disastrous consequences.

2. Compulsory registration criteria

2.1 Introduction

Most people's principal concern relates to the compulsory criteria for registration, and the need to avoid a compliance failure, with the potential result of unexpected VAT liabilities and penalties that follow from that.

There are several "routes" through which compulsory registration can arise. Within each of these there are several points of interpretation which need to be considered in order to draw the correct conclusion at the appropriate time. These are therefore potentially somewhat multi-layered subjects which appear disarmingly simple (as they might be in many cases), but which hide considerable potential complexity.

This book has been laid out on the broad premise that the rules set out first are the ones that are likely to relate to most situations, with decreasingly common scenarios being covered as we progress, though no statistical sampling has been carried out to verify this.

2.2 Who or what must register?

In all of the following cases it is the "person" whose activities are considered compared with the criteria. A "person" is in effect a legal entity carrying out the activities. This person is referred to, throughout this book, as the "entity".

An entity can be a sole proprietor, a partnership, a company of some kind, or any other structure which may be regarded as a legal entity (and some are deemed to be a legal entity where they might not be, such as an English partnership).

With regard to limited partnerships (under the 1907 *Limited Partnerships Act*), it is the "general partner" (or partners) who is deemed to carry on the activity and is thus registered for it, and the limited partners are not regarded as the registered entity. Where a general partner has other activities, these are taken together with the activities of the limited partnership to determine the requirement to register, and any resulting registration covers all his activities including those of the limited partnership. That said,

HMRC comment that limited partnerships cannot own land and property and thus all of the partners (limited or otherwise) might be deemed to form a traditional partnership instead. This is expressed in ambivalent terms, however.

With exceptions which will be explored later, one does not look at the "business", or the "operation" when considering the VAT registration criteria. Thus, for example, if one company carries out two entirely distinct businesses, you must look at both businesses in aggregate in order to apply the registration rules.

2.3 Taxable supplies criteria

For the majority of cases, VAT registration will be required in response to the business making taxable supplies. These rules work on the basis of the value of taxable supplies made, measured in money, which itself is measured in sterling. At the time of writing the threshold was £85,000, and the historic thresholds applicable back to 2011 are given in the Appendix. There are three principal ways in which the criteria are currently engaged:

- where a UK established business exceeds a certain value of taxable supplies made;
- where a foreign business which is not established in the UK exceeds a different (and nil) value of supplies made; and
- where a business becomes aware that it will exceed a certain value of taxable supplies within a prescribed future timeframe.

Note that in each case it is taxable supplies which are relevant, not supplies as such. Exempt supplies are ignored in these tests, as are movements of value which are deemed to be outside the scope of VAT (such as donations and dividends). It is worth considering why that is the case, and this is discussed towards the end of this book in a section dealing with the policy issues surrounding the VAT registration rules. For now, however, it simply has to be accepted that it is taxable, rather than exempt or outside scope, turnover that is relevant.

It is the value of supplies (often called "turnover") that is in point. The value of the profit is completely irrelevant, and a business can be run deliberately at a loss and still be registerable for VAT. But see the section on "agency" for observations as to what counts as "turnover" in some instances.

The *Principal VAT Directive* specifically states that "consideration" includes payments received from third parties towards a supply to a customer. The mere fact that a third party pays for a supply does not stop that being a supply within the scope of VAT.

Taxable supplies include the following classes of supply:

- standard rated
- zero-rated
- reduced rated

Supplies that would be taxable but which are not deemed to be made in the UK, are not included.

Law: VATA 1994, Sch. 1; EC/2006/112

2.3.1 The historic supplies test

This is commonly referred to as the "look back" test.

This requires the entity to consider, at the end of each month, whether, within the preceding 12 months in aggregate, it has exceeded the relevant value of taxable supplies measured in pounds sterling. At the time of writing, this stands at £85,000 (fixed for two years).

It follows that, under this test, as each month goes by, the turnover arising in the equivalent month a year ago falls away from the calculation. It is the "moving annual total", so to speak, which is relevant here.

Any turnover arising in non-sterling currencies therefore needs to be converted at the rate of exchange as at the time of supply. HMRC accept the rate given in national newspapers, but also publish an official rate of exchange. Alternatively, if the entity believes that an alternative rate should apply to it, it can make special application to HMRC, but there would need to be compelling reasons for this to be acceptable.

Whilst the threshold is expressed in purely monetary terms, this does not only refer to the receipt of cash. The "tax point rules" apply to determine when a supply is made, and it is then valued at that time, which may be earlier than the receipt of cash. Payment is not always in monetary terms at all, and can be by way of barter or exchange. These are explored further below.

Certain taxable supplies are always ignored, however, in arriving at the total under this rule. These are supplies of goods or services that are also "capital assets" of the business. But supplies of land and buildings are never regarded as capital assets irrespective of their accounting status, where their supply would be taxable at a positive rate.

Example

Juler Limited is not registered for VAT and sells the freehold of a building which has been used as a centre for providing medical care, and is less than three years old at the time of sale. A building of that age is regarded as "new", and the freehold of a new non-residential building is a standard rated supply. It cannot be ignored because it is an interest in land, and thus adds to the VAT registration total.

On rare occasions, entities may have to consider the operation of this rule in circumstances where they have de-registered from VAT within the last 12 months. In almost all such situations they do not include the turnover that arose while they were previously registered. This is surprising as it seems to create the distortion of allowing an entity which has de-registered (presumably for good reasons) to start with a "clean slate" compared to competing entities that have not been recently VAT registered. The only caveat to this is that HMRC must have been given the correct information when the entity was previously de-registered.

Notification procedure

If, at the end of any given month, the thresholds have been exceeded, the entity has 30 days in which to lodge an application to register for VAT. The compulsory date of registration then becomes the "end of the month" in which notification took place. In practice this means that registrations start on the first of the month following that. To give an example, if the thresholds are exceeded at the end of April, notification must be made by 30 May, and the effective date of registration will be 1 June, unless an earlier date is selected. This means, of course, that all of the taxable turnover that has led towards the breach of the thresholds, and all of the taxable turnover which arises in the month following that breach (subject to the rules below) will not itself be subject to VAT.

Law: VATA 1994, Sch. 1, para. 1

2.3.2 The predicted taxable supplies test

This is known as the "look forward" test.

This requires the entity to consider, at any point in time, whether it knows that it will make taxable supplies to a prescribed value at some point within 30 days which begin on the date of "realisation". It is worth quoting the terms of the legislation in full, since the provisions are not particularly easy to interpret. It requires VAT registration: "at any time if...there are reasonable grounds for believing that the value of these taxable supplies in the period of 30 days then beginning will exceed [value]". This does not require the entity to know that it will make such a value in any given calendar month. The relevant passage of time is from any date to a point in time 30 days later.

As it happens, the value attributed to this threshold has always been the same as the value attributed to the "look back" test. This is inherently confusing. It appears to apply an annual threshold to a 30 day forward looking period. This can give rise to confusion and the mistaken assumption that perhaps only a pro rata amount of that threshold applies (which it does not), or that one has to look forward for a full year (which one does not).

The most common circumstances in which this criterion might arise is where an entity becomes aware that it will make one or perhaps two transactions (within the definitions of a transaction for VAT purposes) within the next 30 days, which, on their own or in aggregate, will exceed the threshold within that period. There appears to be nothing wrong, if this point is realised in advance, in taking steps to avoid the transactions being made in the way that they are initially planned, so as to avoid registration. What is relevant is not the initial plans, but what actually happens, and the expectation that it will happen.

Thus, if an entity had made an arrangement to be paid somewhat in advance of completion of a service, for instance, and wished to have an amount of payment on a particular day which was in excess of the threshold, it might realise that, on that basis, it would be required to register compulsorily for VAT. But it might then decide that it would split the payments such that they did not occur within the same 30 day period, and were both below the registration threshold, and then as long as those payments faithfully represented the true timing of the transactions (on the VAT tax point rules) it would be possible for the expected breach of the threshold to be avoided.

This is important because, under this particular test (as distinct from the "look back" test) there is a requirement to register with effect from the day upon which one became aware of the need to register for VAT under this test. Thus the effective date of registration is the date of realisation, rather than a month or so after that date, or any other later date. What this means is that the transactions that would carry the business over the threshold under this test would be subject to tax, in contrast with the "look back" test where the transactions that carry the entity over the threshold are not actually subject to tax.

Other than this there is a requirement to notify HMRC within 30 days of the realisation occurring.

A question which this begs is, how would anyone realise that he will exceed the threshold in the next 30 days? This matter is not straightforward and the following may assist in interpretation.

Interpreting the "look forward" test

The most difficult thing here is to determine what constitutes "reasonable grounds for believing" that the relevant supplies will be made.

A potentially obvious point is that it is irrelevant as to whether there is a realisation that the provisions of this particular legislation will be engaged as such. Knowledge of the VAT legislation, or the lack of it, is irrelevant in determining whether or not there was an obligation to register. So it is only a question of whether the entity either knew, or had grounds for believing, that the relevant supplies would be made. For this reason, a conscious thought that such a level of supplies was to be made is neither relevant nor likely. If a person does not know the VAT registration rules, he is not going to stop and think that he is about to make supplies above that prescribed level of value. However, he may nonetheless know that he is about to make supplies and what the value of such supplies will be. That, alone, is the necessary knowledge to engage these provisions, irrespective of whether the business is aware of the provisions themselves.

A particular difficulty is that, in most situations, it is almost impossible for supplies to be made to the level in question without the entity knowing that it would do so. This would tempt HMRC to the view that all entities must have known. This will mean that, where it transpires that the relevant quantum of supplies was made in the period, it will be assumed by HMRC that the provisions are engaged on the basis that there must have been reasonable grounds for believing that the supplies would be made. This assumes that supplies cannot be "involuntary".

But, the legislation could then have been framed differently, to cover any situation in which it transpires that supplies to the relevant value have been made in a 30 day period. The fact that it does not do that must mean that there are circumstances in which a business can appear to exceed the threshold without engaging the conditions because it did not have reasonable grounds for believing that the supplies would be made. That can arise in the following situations:

- the supply is passive in delivery (such as royalties arising from an intellectual property right); or
- the entity knows that a taxable supply has been made, but the timing of the supply is the unknown quantity, such as not knowing when a payment will be received for the supply, which in itself could be the action which sets the time of supply for these purposes.

It should therefore not be assumed automatically that because supplies within the 30 day period exceeded the threshold, VAT registration is definitely required from an effective date prior to the making of those particular supplies. That will normally be the case, but not always.

However, it is equally important to note that merely not knowing that supplies were going to be made is insufficient if there were *grounds* for knowing or believing that they would be made. An entity which is blithely unaware of something of which a reasonably conscientious businessman would normally be aware is not defended by his ignorance. Also, the phrase in the legislation is as to whether there are grounds for "believing" that the supplies will be made. This does not require absolute knowledge that they definitely will be made. It may be a point of semantics as to whether it is sufficient to think that the supplies "may" be made, rather than "will" be made. That may be pressing the point rather too far, but clearly the probability of supplies arising seems to fall within the ambit of "reasonable grounds for believing".

Furthermore, it is theoretically possible to believe that the relevant supplies will be made, but for them to fail to materialise. Surreal as it may appear, this would cause the criterion to be met for immediate registration.

It can be seen that the "look forward" test is not an easy one to apply. This, combined with the fact that it is often forgotten (as the "look back" test appears to be more well known and more applicable), means there is room for error to arise.

Law: VATA 1994, Sch. 1, para. 1

2.3.3 The time of supply

In order to interpret these rules, it is important to understand when the value in question is treated as coming into account. Clearly, an entity that has yet to register for VAT cannot issue a "tax invoice" so cannot set a tax point that way. However, it is possible to set a tax point (and thereby a time of supply) by "delivery". If goods are delivered or made available, or services rendered or completed, then in many cases this sets a tax point if the related payment for the supplies has not already been made. This means that the relevant date for VAT registration could be based on delivery to the extent that payment is received later than delivery.

Example

Wright Ltd sells goods worth £100,000 to Bellison Ltd, at a time when the registration threshold is £85,000. Wright Ltd takes a deposit of £25,000, six weeks before delivery. Bellison Ltd then pays the remaining £75,000 three months after delivery.

Assuming that Wright Ltd makes no other supplies, the initial instalment sets a tax point, but for a sum that is not sufficient to breach the thresholds. But the delivery of the goods sets the time of supply to the extent of the remaining price. Wright Ltd cannot wait until it receives the remaining £75,000 before considering registration. It breaches the threshold by virtue of the delivery date for the goods, on the historic supplies basis.

2.3.4 Non-established persons rule

Businesses not established in the UK

Up until 1 December 2012 the above-mentioned rules were applied equally to suppliers who were based entirely outside the UK as to suppliers who had an establishment from which they operate within the UK. However, the CJEU decided (in *Schmelz*) that domestic VAT registration thresholds could not apply to any business that had no establishment in the member state concerned. This was on the footing that member states were unable to monitor activities of a foreign entity so were not able to apply a registration threshold to them.

This logic seems to be fundamentally faulty. First, it is possible to have an establishment for VAT purposes which reports nothing to the member state concerned for direct tax purposes, and does not report to Companies House, so the notion that merely having an establishment on one's soil gives the relevant authorities some kind of extra information does not hold water. Further, merely reducing the registration threshold to "nil" does not magically allow the authorities to detect non-compliance. It is a baffling decision which has wished upon HMRC a regime of extra rules for VAT registration which they could not have wanted and for which they have shown no particular enthusiasm. Nonetheless, we have to operate the rules as best we may, so the question is, how do these rules apply?

The gist of the rules is that there is no target for the value of taxable supplies that has to be attained in order for VAT registration to become mandatory. All that is required is that the entity makes taxable supplies (VATA 1994, Sch. 1A, para. 1).

The following points have to be borne in mind when applying these rules on a practical basis.

- Although there is no monetary target for the value of supplies, there has to be a supply for some kind of consideration, or else these supplies would tend not to be regarded as a business activity. It may therefore be helpful to think in terms of the registration threshold having become 1p rather than "nil".

- The definition of a "non-established" person is one that has "no business establishment or other fixed establishment in the UK". A business establishment is usually regarded as the headquarters, whereas a fixed establishment is a location where there are human and technical resources available to the business. It is not essential that the human resources in question are under employment contracts with the business, as they may be an outsource arrangement. The first step, therefore, in assessing whether this drastically reduced threshold applies to an overseas business is to determine whether it could be said that it has a fixed establishment in the UK; if so, it is then subject to the usual rule, rather than the non-established persons rule.

- This rule does not suspend the usual rules relating to the place of supply, and the potential for the "reverse charge" to apply to imported services, and "acquisition" to apply to goods brought in from another EU state. In other words, if the normal VAT accounting rules require the buyer rather than the seller to account for VAT, on the basis that the seller is not established in the UK, then those rules will continue to apply and the seller does not, by virtue of this particular rule, become registerable for UK VAT. It is therefore only those supplies where the self accounting rules for a purchaser appear not to apply that there is a need to register for UK VAT. Some examples of this situation are referred to below.

- It is possible that a non-established person could start to make taxable supplies shortly before creating a fixed establishment. The rules specifically allow for HMRC to de-register an entity which has been registered under these provisions but which later acquires a fixed establishment in the UK (Sch. 1A, para. 4(2)(b)). This means that the liability to register may well arise for a very brief moment in time between the technical making of a supply and the time of actually setting up an establishment in the UK.

Both the "look forward" and "look back" tests apply to non-established businesses, but in this case there is no actual figure to which to look forward or back. Nonetheless, the legislation includes these tests as though they were separate, and does also provide for different rules relating to the effective date of registration in either case, although it is difficult to see any distinction arising. As mentioned above, where the rules relating to UK established entities are in point, the effective date of registration in respect of the "look back" test is 30 days after the date of breach of the threshold. By contrast, the effective date of registration for a non-established entity is "the beginning of the day on which the liability arises" (para. 5(2)). Thus, if an entity makes a supply it must, within 30 days, notify that fact, and it becomes registerable from that date (that is, the date of the supply), thus catching the supply in the VAT net. However, if the entity can predict that it will make a supply within 30 days, it needs to make notification by the end of that 30 day period, and then HMRC must choose an effective registration date "from the beginning of the period by reference to which the liability arises" (para. 6(2)). Thus, the date of registration becomes the date on which the prediction of the supply was made, which will catch the relevant supply.

Taken all in all, there is no fiscal difference between the "look forward" and "look back" tests in this particular instance. All of those supplies are caught within the VAT net in either case.

Law: VATA 1994, Sch. 1A

Case: *Schmelz v Finanzamt Waldviertel* C-97/09, [2011] STC 88

Practical examples

The question is, in what situations does a non-established person actually make supplies which are not caught by the reverse charge or acquisition accounting which is carried out by his UK customer? These will mainly be:

- goods which are supplied in the UK fulfilled from a stock holding which does not of itself create a fixed establishment;
- provision of goods under a "supply and fit" (or "install & assemble") contract;

- services which are treated as supplied where performed, such as education, but where the customers include private individuals, non-business entities, or perhaps businesses which visit the UK but are not based here;
- certain supplies of land where the customer is likely to be a final consumer, such as the supply of lock-up garages and "self-storage" services;
- supplies related to land made to a consumer which is not VAT registered, such as supplies of architecture or estate agency services;
- provision of certain transport-related services to final consumers;
- broadcasting, telephone, or electronic services for final consumers (though there is an alternative regime: see **2.5.4**).

Place of supply rules following VAT registration

A tricky aspect of the application of the non-established persons rule is what then happens when the entity is required to register for VAT, but its supplies also include those which are subject to a reverse charge.

An example might be that an organisation that provides commercial training to UK companies also provides a small amount of commercial training on a ticketed basis where some of its customers are UK entities which happen not to be carrying on a business (say, museums and libraries). The commercial training provided to the businesses is subject to the reverse charge, and there is no need on that account to register for UK VAT. But the potentially low value supplies made to the occasional museum and library engage the non-established person's VAT registration rule. It is then beyond any doubt that there needs to be a VAT registration but, having become registered, what happens to the liability of the other supplies? Does the non-established business then treat itself as though it belongs in the UK, and thus charges VAT on all of its supplies? Or, conversely, does it take the strict interpretation, treating all services that have been subject to the reverse charge as continuing to be subject to the reverse charge and only charging

VAT on those services where the reverse charge was simply not available?

HMRC take the strict approach. This is interesting and somewhat counterintuitive. It requires the entity to go through the entire rigmarole of registering for UK VAT but then not enjoying the simplification of applying a simple rule across all customers. It has to determine which customers are to be charged VAT and which not. This increases the likelihood of error. It may make an incorrect selection or receive incorrect information from customers upon which it may rely.

It would be more pragmatic, having required an entity to register for VAT, to treat it as though it were a UK-sited business and allow it to apply VAT. That, too, would be better from the point of view of dealing with potential fraud. But, the strict view is what the law requires.

This is an area that may change as time goes by, but clearly it is a difficult rule to apply, and constitutes an unexpected consequence of the CJEU's controversial decision in the first place. Given the potentially large amounts involved in such a distinction it would be appropriate for the entity that faces this point, or its adviser, to obtain a written clearance from HMRC as to the application of this particular rule. In particular, if it presents almost impossible compliance burdens for the business, that point should be made to HMRC to see if they are prepared to apply a different approach.

Guidance: HMRC's *Place of Supply of Services* Manual at VATPOSS 14300

2.4 Transfer of a going concern

2.4.1 Introduction

Transfers of going concerns commonly give rise to the need for the transferee to register for VAT even before he has made a single sale. The idea, here, is that a business, once up and running, should not fall out of the VAT net merely by dint of having being sold from one party to another. Thus, it would not be right for the new owner to be able to await breaching the thresholds in order to be required to register for VAT. The effect of this provision also nullifies any temptation to run a business deliberately in one company for, say, two months, only to transfer it to an associated or commonly owned company for another two months, and so on. The intention behind the legislation is that one looks at the business's track record in order to determine whether VAT registration needs to be, in effect, maintained on that business, rather than the track record of the legal entity itself.

To some extent this is counter-intuitive given that, as discussed above, it is the entity which is registerable rather than the business, but this is a deeming provision which overrides that usual approach.

2.4.2   *TOGCs where no purchase price*

Before going on to the detail, it is worth noting that transfers of going concerns (TOGCs) are notorious for the issues they throw up for VAT. However, most of the issues relate to whether or not the supply is subject to VAT or becomes a "non-supply" by virtue of TOGC status, and if so, what conditions are attached to that. Whilst some of these points may be relevant to the issue of VAT registration, it is all too easy to become confused and to miss the obvious point. That point is that a TOGC can give rise to the need to register for VAT irrespective of some of the other details which may determine whether or not VAT is due on any consideration paid for the business.

Of all of these potential traps, the most significant is the misconception that in order for there to be a TOGC there has to be consideration paid for it. This is not the case. The TOGC can arise without any payment being made by the transferee for the business he receives. Indeed, he may receive a business, together with a payment as an inducement for taking it over, and it would still be regarded, for these purposes, as a TOGC. This means that the provisions relating to registration arising from a TOGC are fully engaged even in those circumstances. This can often be overlooked.

2.4.3   *Inherited turnover rule*

The rules require the transferee to register on the basis of the transferor's turnover in the previous 12 months, as long as the transferor was himself registered or required to be registered. The 12 month period in question is that running up to the date upon which the transfer took place. Thus, if the transfer was on 15 April, the 12 months in question would be the previous 16 April up to 15 April on which the transfer took place. This represents a slight departure from the normal monthly calculation based on a 12 month rolling period.

The way in which the legislation is framed appears somewhat misleading. The reference in Schedule 1 unhelpfully refers to "the value of *his* taxable supplies in the period ..." (para. 1(2)(a), having referred to the *transferee* several times prior to this reference). This appears to produce the nonsensical interpretation that the transferee is supposed to have made the relevant taxable supplies through that particular business in a period 12 months before he even acquired the business. But s. 49 deems the transferee to have received the turnover in such situations and this deeming provision conditions the language in the Schedule, thereby making it intelligible.

It is the previous 12 months' worth of taxable turnover which is relevant, thus excluding any exempt turnover.

Where the transferor transfers only a separately operable part of his business, or a business within a wider portfolio of businesses, one only looks at the turnover generated by that part or that business to determine whether the transferee must immediately register for VAT.

Example

Draper Ltd operates five launderettes and is registered for VAT. It sells the business of one of those launderettes to Brymer Ltd, but that one launderette only turned over £72,000 in the last 12 months prior to transfer. Based on the VAT registration thresholds applicable at the time of writing, Brymer Ltd would not, by virtue of that, need to register for VAT. Draper Ltd may very well turn over several hundred thousand in total, but that is irrelevant.

It is also possible for the transferee to apply to HMRC for waiver of registration, but as this is part of the general scheme of VAT registration, we will deal with it separately.

If these provisions require registration, it becomes applicable from the date of transfer, and thus there is an unbroken liability to VAT.

If, however, the level of historic turnover does not amount to enough to give rise to immediate VAT registration, then the historic turnover must nevertheless continue to be counted as though it were the entity's real turnover for the purpose of the normal "look back" test. Thus, in the above case, Brymer Ltd starts with turnover deemed to be £72,000, which it needs to count towards future potential registration. If, say, the earliest month of that twelve month history shows only £2,000 of turnover, but Brymer Ltd makes £20,000 of turnover in the month following its acquisition of the business, it will be deemed to have turned over £90,000 at that stage and (subject to prevailing thresholds) will need to register. This means Brymer Ltd needs to know that detailed turnover history even if it does not immediately create for Brymer Ltd an obligation to register. It will also need to know it on a monthly basis (rather than from one day to another) as it will then become relevant to the usual "look back" test based on months.

Law: VATA 1994, Sch. 1, para. 1(2)

2.4.4   TOGC "look forward" test

In addition to the "look back" test relating to TOGCs there is a rather curious "look forward" test. This requires the transferee to ask himself whether the business he has just taken over (which presumably does not qualify for compulsory registration under the "look back" test), *will* nonetheless exceed the relevant threshold in the forthcoming 30 day period. It is difficult to see how this is any different to the normal "look forward" provisions for VAT registration, which are dealt with in the preceding section of that schedule. It could be regarded as allowing the knowledge of the transferor to be the relevant knowledge (that is, the transferor happens to know or believe that the business will generate that turnover in the next thirty days following transfer). In that case, however, the legislation should surely use "would" instead of "will", to denote the fact that the transferor cannot hope to make those actual supplies, and in any case the legislation deems the transferee to have the relevant intention. In practice this is hardly important, since it simply provides some kind of double insurance for HMRC.

Law: VATA 1994, Sch. 1, para. 1(1), (2)

2.4.5   TOGC from unregistered transferor

It should be noted that if a business is acquired from an entity that was neither registered nor required to be registered, then the historic turnover is not inherited, and the transferee can start counting his turnover from a nil base.

> **Example**
>
> Mariner Ltd has operated a small vineyard at a turnover of £60,000 per year (and is thus not registered). The company sells it to Bradbury Ltd which intends to combine it with its existing small vineyard that turns over a mere £40,000. In this case, Bradbury Ltd's "history" includes only the £40,000 and not the combined turnover of £100,000.

This seems to be something of an anomaly.

2.4.6 Non-UK established businesses

An important point to note is that this threshold only applies to UK established businesses. There is no assumption that a non-UK established business is to be treated as falling under this rule, and thus able to escape VAT registration if it purchases a business which happens to have taxable supplies below the prevailing VAT registration threshold. In fact, since non-established businesses have no VAT registration threshold (see **2.3.4** above), the TOGC rules are in effect adapted in order to create VAT registration immediately upon acquiring a business, irrespective of how low the taxable turnover of that business is. In other words, the TOGC rules are little short of ephemeral in such cases.

For this reason, it is perfectly possible that a business which has not been VAT registered at any stage during its existence suddenly becomes VAT registered by mere dint of having been acquired as a going concern by a non-established entity. This is the case, not because the TOGC rules are engaged (since they apply only where the transfer is by a person who is or ought to be registered for VAT), but by dint of the nil threshold for the non-established entity.

An example of this might be the acquisition of lock-up garages by an overseas company where the turnover from the garages is, say, £50,000 per year. The provision of parking facilities is generally taxable, but a UK entity which earns this income would not be likely to be registered for VAT. Once it sells the garages, together with the various leases and similar commercial arrangements associated with the garages, to a non-UK established business, the latter is required to register for VAT simply by dint of being non-established. Note that it is irrelevant that the transferor was not already VAT registered. This creates a major incentive for the non-UK entity to create a UK fixed establishment, and it may seek to argue that the agent through which it carries out the activity would be regarded as constituting its fixed establishment (though it would be unlikely to succeed unless the agent had delegated power of decision making).

There are further anomalies where non-established entities are concerned. Since the past turnover generated by a registered business is seemingly irrelevant to the transferee's liability to register in the future, the rules require the business only to register for VAT on the basis of there having been a TOGC if it will make any taxable supplies within the next 30 days. Of course, for most continuing businesses, 30 days is ample for there to be a taxable supply, which would then confirm the TOGC treatment. However, particularly in certain property related contexts, a business could be transferred more than 30 days before the first tax point is set by reference to a charge made for a right over land. On a totally strict reading of the legislation, it is possible then for the TOGC provisions not to bite upon the non-established entity. Of course, this means nothing more, at the most, than that VAT registration will be delayed for another few days, rather than taking place at the date of the transfer. The only point, therefore, is as to whether the basis of registering the non-established person is under what one might call an "intending trader" basis, or under the more logical TOGC basis.

HMRC have clarified their views on this R&C Brief 11(2016) as follows:

Where the situation involves a lease of property, or any arrangement where "rent" or period-related charges are made, and the seller makes such a charge in advance of the transfer of the business as to cover a period of more than 30 days of the buyer's custody of the business, they view the buyer as making supplies in that 30 day period, which means that there is a TOGC. This is a questionable interpretation, but there appear to be no practical problems with it.

The same Brief clarifies that, where the "period charge" concept does not apply (such as where a shop shuts for a refurbishment after acquisition), and the next supply is more than 30 days after the transfer, this is not a TOGC for VAT registration purposes. In that case the overseas based buyer needs to apply for VAT registration voluntarily if it is to be registered with effect from the date of the transfer. However, HMRC confirm that, if the buyer applies for such a registration prior to the transfer date, they will allow the seller to treat the supply as a TOGC for the purposes of the "non-supply" rules. That last point does not bear on the issue of the registration, but it is, of course, of great importance for both the seller and buyer and needs to be attended to as part of the wider picture.

Law: VATA 1994, Sch. 1A, para. 2

2.4.7   Defining a TOGC

All of the above assumes that one knows when one has taken over a going concern. This in itself is a fairly substantial subject, which is often determined by non-VAT related issues.

As already mentioned, a TOGC does not arise, technically, unless the transferor was registered or was required to be registered.

There can sometimes be a debate between taxpayers and HMRC as to the degree of latitude that can be afforded to the concept of a "TOGC".

A key distinction may be that HMRC will expect to see the "same kind of business" being carried on by the transferee as by the transferor. HMRC say that, for instance, a catering business can change quite substantially but still be "the same kind of business", if what is carried on is a catering business of some kind. However, it is far from clear that a business which sells goods can be transferred with stock, and be regarded by HMRC as "the same kind of business" if the transferee only ever leases the goods, thus no longer carrying out a selling operation. Furthermore, where a business operates its activity "in hand" then a transfer to a transferee who intends to make charges to another party to operate the business (such as a franchisee) would generally be regarded by HMRC as constituting a different business, and therefore not a TOGC. These are highly debatable points. For the person who wishes to avoid compulsory VAT registration, HMRC's more narrow approach (than appears to be supported by the case authorities on TOGCs in general) can actually be helpful.

It stands to reason, however, that any transferee (or his adviser) will wish to obtain an HMRC determination in respect of his obligations to register, rather than merely relying on the assumption that the business he intends to operate is sufficiently different from the one that he purchased.

HMRC tend to overlook relatively brief closures of a business (in order to refurbish them) when considering TOGC treatment, so it would not be possible for a transferee to deny that TOGC VAT registration treatment applies to him if he has merely shut the business for reasonable refurbishment. However, if he has taken over a business which has definitely ceased, albeit it may within the previous 12 months have generated more than the requisite turnover, he would be able to argue that there is no TOGC to start with, and that these conditions are therefore not engaged.

A further point of detail is the treatment of sales of capital assets. A business may have sold capital assets in the preceding 12 months before being transferred, but these are specifically ignored when determining the turnover that the business has generated in that period. That of course is logical, but the rule does not apply to the disposal by the transferor of a right over land.

This replicates the conditions regarding registering for VAT on the basis of the turnover achieved by a business from start-up, but it is impossible to discern any good policy reason as to why this rule applies under the TOGC treatment. After all, the seller will have accounted for any VAT that is relevant on such taxable supplies while the business was registered. It cannot give rise to an appropriate appraisal of the ongoing turnover generated by a business when the transferee takes it over. This therefore appears to be a somewhat misconceived use of a provision which is out of place. That said, since the transferee can apply for exemption from registration under the predicted supplies test (discussed later) the point may have little practical impact.

Law: VATA 1994, Sch. 1, para. 1(7), (8)

2.4.8 Transfer of existing VAT number

Where registration arises as a consequence of a TOGC, there is a choice available to the parties to choose to transfer the existing VAT number of the business to the new owner. This is not compulsory

Compulsory registration criteria

and is almost never undertaken, since it brings with it liability for all of the potential VAT debts of the previous business owner, an obligation that a sensible person would resist in almost all circumstances. It is also only possible where the transferor of the business intends to cease taxable activity entirely (which, of course, is often not the case).

The sole apparent benefit of transferring the number is that it also confirms an absolute right to recover the input tax that the previous owner may have omitted to claim or to benefit from refunds of tax overpaid by the previous owner. However, there are other grounds for arguing that such rights transfer without the need to transfer the VAT number, and legal advice should be taken on how to improve one's chances of these applying without taking on the burden of liability for any previous under-payments.

As a general rule of thumb, the choice of transferring the number of the transferor should be rejected.

2.5 Further grounds for registration arising from international activity

2.5.1 Acquisition of goods from EU

The acquisition of goods from the EU arises from two possible scenarios:

- buying the goods from a stock situated elsewhere in the EU;
- transferring one's own goods from an EU site to the UK.

The mere act of carrying out acquisitions can give rise to the liability to register for VAT.

However, this basis does not apply where the acquisition is made pursuant to making a taxable supply of the goods themselves. It follows that, where the acquired goods are to be sold on a supply which is generically taxable, registration does not arise under this rule. This presumably reflects the fact that the other reasons for VAT registration will potentially apply.

Accordingly, the provision applies where the acquired goods are to be used for an exempt or non-business purpose. It does not apply, however, where any taxable use of the goods is to be made, even, apparently, where non-taxable use is also present. There appears also to be no requirement *per se* to re-supply the goods at market value in order to replicate the values-based criteria of the other registration criteria, or to make taxable supplies using such goods which are sold at open market value.

As the legislation excludes any acquisition "in pursuance of a taxable supply", an arising question is as to whether one must have a concrete and certain taxable use intention at the time of the acquisition to be able to disregard it. This does appear to require an actual intention of that kind at the time of acquisition if it is to be regarded as "pursuant" to a future taxable supply. It seems to follow that the acquisition of goods for uncertain kinds of use cannot be disregarded under this rule. On a practical level, however, that uncertainty is unlikely to arise.

This rule applies to non-business use by an entity other than a natural person (an individual) if he is to use the goods privately.

The thresholds are the same as for the making of actual taxable supplies. However, unlike the reverse charge situation, where the importation of services is deemed to be a supply made by the importer, acquisitions are treated as a special category of "taxable event", not as proxy supplies. The consequence is that VAT registration only applies where the acquisitions themselves exceed that value, not where the acquisitions, combined with any other activity, exceed the value.

A further aspect of this rule is that, whilst a "look back" test is applied, it only looks back to 1 January of the calendar year, and not to the previous 12 months. Therefore, at the end of every month, a person must look back over all of the months of the calendar year in question, and determine whether the aggregate value of acquisitions exceeds the threshold.

Having triggered the need to register for VAT on the "look back" test, notification has to be made to HMRC within 30 days, and the VAT registration has effect from the first day of the month following that. For example, if the threshold is exceeded at the end of April, the application for VAT registration has to be lodged by 30 May, and the VAT registration becomes effective from 1 June. This, therefore, closely mirrors the normal VAT registration application process for the "look back" test.

There is also a "look forward" test. This works the same as with the normal "look forward" test. The entity has to consider whether "at any time there are reasonable grounds for believing that the value of his acquisitions in the period of 30 days then beginning will exceed [the threshold]". See **2.3.2** for discussion of the interpretation of this language.

Again, as with the "look forward" test generally, the effective date of registration is the beginning of the period through which the liability arose, and thus VAT registration catches the relevant transaction. Again, as with the general "look forward" test, it coincidentally has a threshold which is identical to the annual threshold for the "look back" test.

In practical terms, relatively few businesses will fall to be registered compulsorily under these provisions. In particular, however, it can affect exempt businesses that happen to purchase goods from elsewhere in the EU. Of course, the supply of goods from a supplier elsewhere in the EU to a non-VAT registered UK business would be subject to local VAT in the supplier's state. However, the purchaser becomes registered for VAT once the value of the transactions exceeds the above thresholds, and the sales to that purchaser would then revert to being zero-rated by the supplier. From that point the UK business has to charge itself VAT on the value of the acquisition, and will be unable to claim the VAT.

Law: VATA 1994, Sch. 3, para. 1

Failure to recognise need to register

The question this begs is, what happens when transactions are not covered by the zero rate for the seller (since the VAT registration of the purchaser has not yet been achieved), but the sales in question are subject to acquisition tax in the UK because the effective date of VAT registration has already arisen under these rules? There is no obvious answer to this. When the business is deploying the "look back" test, there is a period of grace in which it can make arrangements for all supplies from the effective date of registration to become zero-rated by furnishing the supplier with the VAT registration number it has recently acquired. This, however, assumes that HMRC can process the VAT registration application sufficiently promptly to provide the number. That is actually unlikely, given the restricted timeframes. One can only trust, therefore, that an application can be made to the supplier to reverse his VAT charge on the basis of receiving a VAT registration number belatedly. However, this creates risk for the supplier on the basis that he cannot necessarily know the date from which the VAT registration number was valid. It can be expected that a supplier will wish to take steps to verify the date of validity of the VAT registration number by reference to inspecting VAT registration certificates and making enquiries through information channels in his own state as to the *bona fides* of the situation.

This is exacerbated where the "look forward" test applies, since the very transaction upon which the seller will have charged local VAT, will be the one that takes the UK-based acquiring company over the threshold, which, under those rules, will then include that particular acquisition within the effective date of registration. Double taxation seems to be a virtual certainty in those situations. Again, one can only hope that the supplier will understand the position and be willing to accept a belated notification of the VAT registration number in order to credit the VAT charge retrospectively.

The biggest danger, of course, is where the purchaser fails completely to notice the need to register and thus continues to pay the supplier's VAT charge on acquisitions long after he ought to have been registered. It may be tempting for the entity to think that, having been charged VAT by the supplier, he cannot be expected to owe VAT to HMRC as well. That is incorrect, however. HMRC will want to receive the VAT revenues, rather than ceding them to another member state, and will demand the VAT. At that stage the supplier is likely to be completely unwilling to rescind the VAT charges. Double taxation (with the ignominy of penalties in addition) is the likely result.

Valuation of acquisition

Helpfully, there is a provision which ensures that the VAT charged on such transactions prior to the registration being required, is not itself regarded as part of the value of the supply which could trigger registration under this basis (VATA 1994, Sch. 3, para. 1(5)).

Example

A Danish entity makes a supply of goods of £70,000 to a UK entity, on which it charges Danish VAT at 25%. The full transaction value is £87,500. However, £17,500 of this is Danish VAT.

The value for the purposes of registration is only £70,000. At the time of writing, this was below the threshold. If nothing more arises, this would not trigger the need to register for VAT on the basis of acquisition of goods.

It is tempting to think that it would be better to be registered for VAT in order to pay a lower rate of VAT upon acquisition (20% in the UK at the time of writing). That may perhaps be true, but the UK business could also be carrying out a certain level of UK taxable activity (albeit unconnected with this taxable activity), but below the threshold, and would not wish to bring that within range of a substantive VAT charge simply in order to achieve a slightly lower rate of VAT upon acquisitions.

Since the acquisition threshold stands separately from any other threshold, it has the potential, single-handedly, to create an unwanted VAT liability on taxable supplies which are sheltered by the usual VAT registration threshold. Clearly, this should be considered at the planning stage when deciding whether to procure from the EU or procure from the UK.

There are provisions to register voluntarily for acquisitions of goods and this is discussed in **Chapter 9**.

Law: VATA 1994, Sch. 3, para. 1(5)

2.5.2   *Distance selling liability*

It should be noted that the information in this section relates to rules which are under review by the EU at the time of writing, with the potential intention of introducing a "MOSS" based system as described in section **2.5.4** (currently relating only to electronic services). Readers should check the latest position before reviewing the following.

A separate free-standing obligation to register for VAT arises where a supplier carries out "distance selling" of goods to non-business customers. This mainly applies to businesses based in other EU territories which carry out mail order (including internet order) activities into a target market in the UK. However, by the same token, a UK business can suffer from the need to register for VAT under "distance selling" in any other EU state into which it makes distance sales. Note that this relates only to goods and not to services.

From this point onwards, we concentrate only on the impact for overseas EU businesses selling into the UK.

Much like the acquisitions rule, this particular rule is based on the value of supplies made in any calendar year. This is therefore different to deploying the 12-month rolling period test of the normal VAT registration rules. Unlike any other test, this one is based on an entirely different figure, which at the time of writing was £70,000. Again unlike any other test, this is not based upon consideration of the monthly position, but arises on the day at which the total relevant sales exceed the threshold. The result of this is that the business is obliged to consider daily the question of whether it has breached the threshold, rather than doing so only at the end of each month.

Thus there is only a "look back" test, and no "look forward" test (VATA 1994, Sch. 2, para. 1).

Having exceeded the threshold, an entity needs to notify HMRC of the liability within 30 days. It will then become registerable with effect from the very day on which it exceeded the threshold, unless it elects to become registerable at an earlier date (Sch. 2, para. 3).

It is difficult to see how anyone would wish to backdate the VAT registration at that stage, since it would have accounted for domestic VAT on those sales with little chance of being able to recoup it from the local tax authority. It is actually possible to register voluntarily for "distance selling" into a country (see **9.7**). Therefore, the likely chosen treatment would be for the date of compulsory registration to be adopted in a situation where the business had waited until it had exceeded the threshold in order to notify the requirement to account for UK VAT.

The value of taxable supplies which gives rise to this obligation is the net of VAT value, not the gross retail value.

Example

Klocker GmbH of Germany sells goods into the UK to a sterling equivalent value of £75,000 but accounts to the German authorities for £12,000 (rounded). In this case Klocker GmbH has made sales of only £63,000 which (at the time of writing) was not sufficient to require registration under this provision.

However, there is a "nil" threshold in respect of distance sales of goods subject to excise duties, or a "new means of transport" such as a new car.

Definition of "distance selling"

The next question, then, is: what constitutes "distance selling" so that we can recognise when we might have exceeded the threshold?

There are several specific conditions set out in the legislation (Sch. 2, para. 10), all of which have to be met:

1. the supply involves the removal of the goods to the UK by, or under the directions of, the supplier;
2. the supply does not involve the installation or assembly of the goods at a place in the UK;
3. the supply is a transaction in pursuance of which the goods are acquired in the UK from another EU member state by a person who is not "a taxable person" in regard to the UK;
4. the supply forms part of a "business"; and
5. the supply is not an exempt supply; nor is it a supply which is subject to excise duty or is classified as a "new means of transport" (since these two classes of supply are governed by special rules giving them a "nil" threshold for distance selling registration).

The interpretation of this is mainly fairly obvious, but the interesting one, perhaps, is the concept of the supply involving "the removal of the goods by or under the directions of the supplier". Thus the goods have to be in a place outside the UK, and must have been removed (that is to say started upon their physical journey) either by the supplier, or under his particular directions. But, if the goods are moved by the customer, or by an agent of the customer, then it would not appear that these conditions are engaged.

Of course, most agents in such situations would actually acquire the goods in the course of their business, and then account for UK VAT upon the sale, thus effectively negating the need for the "distance selling" regulations altogether. But this might not be the case where an independent-minded customer, or group of customers, privately decided to arrange the transport alone. Furthermore, it is not clear that facilitation of that arrangement by the supplier necessarily has to go so far that the supplier is regarded as providing the directions for the removal of the goods. Thus, a supplier can go to a considerable extent to facilitate the goods being moved on behalf of the customer, as long as the customer is the party that finally directs their movement. Clearly the person carrying out the movement or removal cannot be the supplier himself, as he will then be caught, but it could be, for example, an associated company of his.

The question of artificiality cannot be ignored in this regard. HMRC could take the view that revenues are under attack by arrangements that are only contemplated to save VAT (albeit they are probably as much to do with administrative ease), and they may take action accordingly.

Turning briefly to the situation where a UK business may be caught by "distance selling" in other EU states, it is worth noting that certain products are zero-rated in the UK, whereas they are subject to positive rates of tax in those other countries, so avoiding having to register for "distance selling" in those other countries could produce a much improved fiscal outcome. That said, the UK is unusual in having such a high threshold of £70,000, and most of the EU states operate on the basis of something of the order of €35,000.

Law: VATA 1994, Sch. 2

2.5.3   VAT-claimed goods

There is a special set of rules relating to businesses which are based outside the UK but which claim VAT on goods acquired within the UK under what is called the "13th directive" regime, or the equivalent rules for non-UK EU businesses. This is a regime for overseas businesses that incur VAT in the course of furtherance of a business which would be taxable if it had been carried on in the UK, to reclaim VAT so as not to be burdened unfairly.

The majority of cases where such VAT is claimed involve services rather than goods. However, given that goods can occasionally be involved, there is a rule that effectively requires the purchaser of such VAT-claimed goods to register for VAT if it sells the goods on a "taxable supply". In essence this means that the goods would have to be in the UK at the time of sale and not intended for export (which would make them zero-rated and therefore of no concern). Thus, if an overseas business without an establishment in the UK sells goods on which it has reclaimed VAT, it must register for UK VAT in order to account for VAT on that particular sale.

There is no value threshold for this, nor is there any delay in the effective date of VAT registration. Thus, in theory at least, heavily depreciated goods could be sold for scrap value within the UK and still be required to be covered by a VAT registration for the sole purpose of accounting for VAT on such sales. It seems unlikely, however, that this rule is observed in practice in all but a minority of situations.

There is a further complication. The same principle applies if an overseas company sells goods which it acquired as part of a transfer of an undertaking (transfer of a going concern) where VAT was not charged to it, and where the transferor had claimed the VAT on the goods under the same mechanism. Hence, where a non-UK based business purchases goods that are situated in the UK from another such business which had made the claim, it needs to require the seller to provide information about the goods that fall within that category in order to comply with the VAT registration requirements arising from this rule.

Except where this provision might have some use to attack contrived avoidance schemes (or more sensibly, to stop them in their tracks), it is hard to believe that it has any practical application at all. However, the rules should not be ignored.

Law: VATA 1994, Sch. 3A, para. 9

2.5.4 Electronic services

Since 1 January 2015, all B2C supplies of "electronic services" have been covered by what is colloquially called the Mini One Stop Shop ("MOSS").

The principle behind this is that any supplier, wherever he is based, accounts for VAT to the member state in which his non-business customer belongs, rather than where the supplier himself belongs. To achieve this the supplier must determine where each customer belongs.

The supplier can choose to register for VAT in each separate EU state, or can choose the MOSS alternative. To ease the burden of multiple VAT registrations and submissions, only one VAT registration (under MOSS) is required to deal with most of those obligations.

For organisations with a single fixed establishment in the UK, all of these supplies of such electronic services to UK-based consumers fall under their normal VAT return. For supplies to other EU countries, they can apply to register under MOSS. They submit a MOSS return for the combined sales to those countries, but itemising each country's sales separately, and the VAT thereon. They make a single payment to HMRC to process the MOSS return, and partition the payment between each member state.

A UK business with more than one fixed establishment, say one in the UK and others elsewhere in the EU, registers, and accounts, for VAT in the conventional way for any state in which it has a fixed establishment. However, it can separately nominate one of those states (usually the one where the headquarters or business establishment is situated) as the place for making the MOSS return.

Businesses based wholly outside the EU may simply nominate one state in which they would register under MOSS and would make the relevant MOSS submission. Member states charge commission to the other member states for partitioning the payment to them where the non-EU business is involved.

Dependent on the details of the "Brexit" settlement under which the UK looks destined to leave the EU, the UK becomes a "third country" and no longer operates MOSS from the relevant date. However, UK businesses will need to apply MOSS by choosing a host EU state to register for the relevant purpose. It is expected that the UK will introduce complementary rules to tax B2C electronic services in the place of consumption, thus requiring registration for UK VAT of all overseas businesses that sell such services to UK-sited consumers.

Where the supply is to a business customer (B2B) the place of supply is where the customer belongs. But supplies of electronic and telecoms services are deemed to be made in the UK if a non-EU business customer "uses and enjoys" the supply in the UK. This overrides the normal rule which taxes B2B supplies in the customer's place of establishment. The effect can be that an overseas-based supplier of electronic services which are used and enjoyed in the UK, albeit supplied to a person based outside the EU, is required to register for UK VAT under the place of supply rules.

In respect of the MOSS system for B2C supplies, there is no turnover threshold, but on the other hand the language of the provision shows that it is a matter of choice as to whether the non-EU established business registers under these provisions.[1] The reason for this is that the only alternative to a non-EU based entity would be to register in each EU country in which it had such customers. Thus, MOSS is a facilitation measure which allows registration to occur in only one country as a proxy for the rest. To that extent, it is not compulsory, but voluntary, though it deals with the issue in the context of an obligation to register.

It was recognised (somewhat belatedly) that the effect of there being no threshold for registering under MOSS, and no threshold for registering separately in each member state, was to drag micro-businesses into VAT registration where they otherwise would be below the conventional UK registration thresholds. At first, salt was added to this wound by the requirement that MOSS traders be UK VAT registered, such that all UK sales would then be subject to imposition of UK VAT despite the businesses being below the threshold, with only the choice to pursue separate registration in all target states as a "solution" to that problem. However, this was rectified shortly after the inception of MOSS by maintaining the requirement to register both for UK VAT and MOSS, but allowing traders not to account for VAT on UK supplies as long as the value of these supplies was below the UK threshold.

In addition, the UK indicated that they would regard micro-businesses with very low turnovers as arguably not being in business at all and thus (on that interpretation) not subject to any

---

[1] VATA 1994, Sch. 3B, para. 2 refers to the fact that the person "may" be registered under the Schedule.

VAT registration regime. These compromises have created the impression of a regime that has more than its fair share of complexities which have been given insufficient consideration in the context of small businesses.

The EC Commission has proposed a €10,000 threshold be introduced in 2018.

MOSS applies to the following electronic services:

- supplies of images or text, such as photos, screensavers, e-books and other digitised documents (e.g. PDF files);
- supplies of music, films and games, including games of chance and gambling games, and programmes on demand;
- online magazines;
- website supply or web hosting services;
- distance maintenance of programmes and equipment;
- supplies of software and software updates;
- advertising space on a website.

It also applies to broadcasting and telecommunications services, including:

- the supply of audio and audio-visual content for simultaneous listening or viewing by the general public on the basis of a programme schedule by a person that has editorial responsibility;
- live streaming through the internet if broadcast at the same time as transmission by radio or television;
- fixed and mobile telephone services for the transmission and switching of voice, data and video, including telephone services with an imaging component, otherwise known as videophone services;
- telephone services provided through the internet, including Voice over Internet Protocol (VoIP);
- voice mail, call waiting, call forwarding, caller identification, 3-way calling and other call management services;

- paging services;
- access to the internet.

But the key point of definition is that the services are supplied with no, or minimal, human involvement. In essence, once the service has been set up, it proceeds completely automatically. For this reason, a service that has a large digital/electronic component, but needs human intervention to operate, is not regarded as an electronic supply for the purposes of MOSS.

These place of supply rules also mandate requirements relating to determining where the customer is established. These are highly detailed, and readers are advised to refer to the HMRC guidance (see below) for the detailed current guidance.

Law: VATA 1994, Sch. 3B

Guidance: HMRC's *VAT: businesses supplying digital services to private consumers*

3. Defining "supplies"

3.1 Situations regarded as supplies

Since VAT registration is based on "supplies" made by the entity, this begs the question as to how one determines when supplies have been made. The following examples help to illustrate what is or what is not a supply, or what the value of the supply could be. This issue needs to be explored in some depth to avoid a mishap.

3.2 Barter

Barter is where, without using any monetary value, or exchange of money in any form, one party agrees to do something for another party in return for that party doing something for it. This can be a barter of goods, or of services, or a mixture of these.

Example

Garside Ltd agrees to paint the premises of Thurston Ltd, in return for Thurston Ltd providing an interest free loan to Garside Ltd. This is a two-way transaction. Garside Ltd has provided a decorating service which is taxable. Thurston Ltd has provided credit which is an exempt supply.

The position is exacerbated in this case by the fact that Thurston Ltd presumably cannot reclaim VAT, because it is making exempt supplies. It is tempting to ignore the barter and to say that there has been no supply by either party. This is incorrect. There is a value to the painting job, and if that value, together with any other monetary transactions carried out by Garside Ltd, exceeds the threshold, then it must register for VAT and in due course account for VAT accordingly. Thurston Ltd makes an exempt supply so that does not trigger the need for it to register for VAT, but the value of its exempt supply is, objectively speaking, the interest it forgoes in consideration of receiving the "free" decorating service. In theory the value of the decorating service should be identical to the value of the interest forgone on the loan.

The "tax point" for the decorating service would be deemed to be the date on which the service is completed, unless any consideration was paid during the course of the job. That could be the case here

Defining "supplies"

because it may be that the first payment of interest which is not charged would arise part way through the job, thus crystallising a value. However, if that would not be true until after the job was completed, then the time of supply is the date of completion of the job itself.

Accordingly, all of the value of the interest which is not to be charged could be regarded as the proxy value for the decorating service. Since the decorating service would have been completed for VAT purposes at that point in time, it is the entire rolled up value of the interest forgone by Thurston Ltd which would be regarded as the value applicable to Garside Ltd's decoration service at that point in time (or the equivalent net present value). It is possible, however, that Garside Ltd could try to substitute a genuine market value for the decorating service if it believes this is lower than the interest which Thurston Ltd decides to forgo. HMRC might want to know why it would be lower, and why that would be a reasonable bargain for Thurston Ltd to strike, but that, at least, is a point that can be argued in Garside Ltd's favour if it would produce a better result.

However, assuming that either the value of Garside Ltd's services or the value of the interest forgone by Thurston Ltd amounts to something in excess of the VAT registration thresholds (or, does if combined with Garside Ltd's other monetary turnover) then either the "look forward" or the "look back" test may be engaged by this interaction.

The point is extremely easily missed. HMRC did not notice it in the case of *Storer* in which the Tribunal held that two seaside caterers bartered by exchanging alcoholic drinks for portions of fish and chips, thus creating mutual taxable supplies (which HMRC had wrongly thought were mere private use of the goods).

Case: *MG & ND Storer v HMRC* [2017] UKFTT 776 (TC)

3.3 Face value vouchers

This book does not cover the myriad complexities of face value vouchers, but it should be noted that many face value vouchers do not create a "supply" when they are "sold". They are treated as being merely an exchange of cash. The supply comes when they are redeemed. But there are complex exceptions, so any business that is involved in vouchers of this kind will need to refer to guidance on this topic and then apply those rules to the registration requirements.

3.4 Imported services

A common oversight is the failure to understand the counter-intuitive rule that, where services that are subject to the "reverse charge" are imported, the value of the imported services is treated as a value of taxable supplies made by the importer (at least as regards certain classes of such services). This only applies where the imported services are themselves taxable. This is rooted in the fact that imported services are deemed to be taxable supplies made by the importer.

In practice there are very few services when imported from an overseas entity that are not subject to the reverse charge if imported by a UK entity. However, whilst most services are subject to reverse charge accounting when imported by a VAT-registered entity, the range of services that give rise to the need for their importer to register on the basis that the purchases are deemed to be taxable supplies is narrower.

Law: VATA 1994, s. 8

Excluded imported services

The services that are *excluded* from this regime (when considering the registration rules on their own) are ones listed in VATA 1994, Sch. 4A. These need to be considered in detail in each case, but are broadly as follows:

- land related supplies;
- passenger transport;
- hire of means of transport;
- cultural, educational, and entertainment services;
- catering;
- hiring of goods;
- transport of goods;
- electronic and telecoms services.

Hence, all other services when supplied to a UK established entity, acting in furtherance of its business, are covered by the reverse charge where the effect is that the supply is deemed to arise in the UK.

Example

A UK business entity which is in start-up mode, or which is largely exempt and thus not registered, imports a service from abroad and is thus not charged UK VAT. The likelihood is that this import value will be considered to be a value of taxable supplies made by the importing entity.

By definition, this cannot apply to non-established entities, since they cannot be deemed to import a service because they do not have an establishment in the UK. It also does not apply where the service is provided by another division of the same legal entity as the importer (subject to a potential exception effective from January 2016 where that overseas division is part of a VAT group in some – not all – EU member states, and which is covered in R&C Brief 18(2015)). Nor does it apply where the service is not to be used for the business purposes of the importer.

Practical example

A common example of this problem might be as follows: a UK entity, Willman Ltd, makes taxable supplies to a value of £60,000 per year and its other supplies are exempt from VAT.

Willman Ltd wishes to license its corporate identity to an overseas operation. By way of preparation, it commissions two services, one a consultancy service from a supplier in the jurisdiction in question and the other a legal service from that same jurisdiction. Both of these service providers will not be charging either UK VAT or local VAT because the services are such as should be self-accounted under the reverse charge.

Assume that the fees in aggregate are £30,000. Willman Ltd thus imports £30,000 of such services, producing an annual aggregate taxable turnover of £90,000 (£60,000 + £30,000) for that year. This exceeds the UK VAT registration threshold (at the time of writing), meaning that Willman Ltd will need to register for UK VAT, probably under the look-back test. The look-forward test could also be engaged, of course, if the figures were higher than this.

Law: VATA 1994, s. 8

Barter interaction with reverse charge

This, of course, can also be combined with the difficulty entailed in "barter". Say the UK entity can provide something of benefit to the overseas lawyer, and they agree to swap services. It is tempting to think that there is no VAT registration connotation here. If the services provided to the overseas lawyer are themselves treated as "outside the scope of UK VAT", or would otherwise be exempt from VAT, then those services of themselves do not give rise to the need to register for UK VAT on the part of their supplier. But imported services, to which no clear monetary value is attached, could do, as they would be regarded as the making of taxable supplies in the UK. Therefore barter, combined with the reverse charge, creates a potential timing problem for VAT registration.

Exceptions to reverse charge registration

However, the exceptions to the reverse charge registration treatment can create scenarios where UK VAT registration does not impact on the importer. For example, if a UK based supplier of residential rental property imports an estate agent's service in relation to a UK property he intends to purchase, then the rule is not engaged, as this service is excluded from the VAT registration remit by being included in Schedule 4A. However, in that case the non-UK established agent has a liability to register for and charge the VAT.

Another exception might be where a business based solely in another EU state, but with residential rental properties in the UK, commissions a non-UK property consultancy to prepare a report on the general UK "property scene" to help inform future choices. The service imported is not one that relates to "land" (being insufficiently precise in its relationship with specific sites) and thus is of the type that might have necessitated registration on importation. However, the business that imports it is actually established outside the UK (assuming that this is the case under the establishment rules), and the result is that it imports the service into the country in which it is established, and not into the UK. Thus, despite the business in question relating to UK sources of income, there is no basis on which the recipient of the services is registerable for UK VAT.

3.5 Self supplies

3.5.1 *Introduction*

"Self supplies" are often overlooked as a potential source of the need to declare VAT where no actual supply has taken place, or indeed to register for VAT. In truth, most "self supplies" are derived from cases where a certain amount of VAT has been reclaimed on a purchase, and then it is used in some other way. That situation does not normally apply to a non-VAT registered person. But there are exceptions which could also trap the unwary unregistered person.

3.5.2 *Construction*

A supply is deemed to arise where an organisation uses its own staff to provide itself with construction services where the open market value of the services would be £100,000 or more. Strictly speaking, this applies even to cases where the business could reclaim any VAT that was charged to it by an external contractor. It is clear that the purpose of the provision is to catch situations where the business is partly or wholly exempt, and thus cannot reclaim all or any of its VAT on costs. The self supply generates a charge to VAT which it cannot reclaim or cannot fully reclaim. But, the rule operates such that the fully taxable business is also "caught" by the mechanism of the self supply. In extreme circumstances this could mean that an embryonic business may provide itself with facilities by using its own construction staff long before it actually makes any taxable supplies and thus triggers the need to register for VAT at that earlier stage as determined by the self supply rules. However, the major threat is for those businesses which are established, but are making exempt supplies. These will tend to be in the academic and educational areas, care, medical supplies, gambling establishments, and perhaps undertakers. The most likely victim of this situation would probably be the care homes sector.

The circumstances in which it can arise are basically as follows. First, since the business has to provide itself with construction services, it will be using its employed staff to carry out construction work, the outcome of which it will then use for its own business. Construction work includes the following:

- the construction of a building;
- the extension or alteration of a building where the additional floor area is not less than 10% of the original floor area;
- construction of an annex which adds 10% or more to the floor area;
- civil engineering construction;
- consequent demolition as part of a scheme of construction.

Construction services are deemed to be subject to VAT at the time that they are completed (where, as inevitably in this case, no consideration is paid). Thus, the time of the supply for the purposes of VAT registration will be the completion of a particular piece of work which gives rise to a particular new building, new civil engineering work, or new extension. Since the minimum value to "trigger" this self supply liability is significantly greater than the current VAT registration threshold (at the time of writing), it follows that the supply would be predictable and would be caught under the "look forward" test for VAT registration (see above). Accordingly, VAT registration would be notified within 30 days of the business becoming aware that it would exceed the threshold by virtue of the self supply. The registration would start with effect from the date upon which the entity became aware of the position (that is, before the date the self supply itself occurs). This means that any self supply that triggers the liability to register for VAT will, itself, bear VAT, to the disadvantage of the partly exempt business.

It is surprising that self supply is still on the statute books. It would be more relevant if there was a self supply of internally provided legal or consultancy services as an alternative, or perhaps in addition, to this particular self supply. It does appear to discriminate against organisations which happen to find it more cost effective to employ their own construction workforce. In the new world of reductions to "red tape", this would appear to be a rule that ought to be abolished straightaway. By the time you read this book, it might have been, so you should check whether it is still on the statute books.

Law: SI 1989/472

3.5.3 Charities and residential providers

Charities and providers of certain kinds of residential facilities (such as student accommodation) often benefit from a VAT relief on the construction of buildings for "relevant charitable purposes" and "relevant residential purposes". As an anti-avoidance provision, the law requires them to use the building on which no VAT has been charged to them for at least ten years for the restricted qualifying use. If, within that time, they transgress the boundaries, a self supply occurs and they would be liable to register if the value exceeded the thresholds.

The specific rules relating to these provisions are complex and should be researched in a publication dedicated either to charities/residential or to construction (or on HMRC's website), but the point needs to be borne in mind. It is tempting to think that the self-supply can only bite if the entity is already registered but that is not the case, and would defeat the point of the measure. Admittedly, any charity or similar entity that finds itself in this position has almost certainly made an expensive error, since the rules usually have the effect of ensuring that the restricted use is adhered to, but this does not stop the rule being applicable where it oversteps that line.

Law: VATA 1994, Sch. 10

3.6 Supply valuation

Surprisingly, VAT registration appears not to be in point where HMRC might wish to direct that an open market value applies to supplies between related parties where the customer cannot reclaim its input tax. VATA 1994, Sch. 6, Pt. 2 gives HMRC a power in such cases to direct that a charge at under value between related parties is to be revalued for VAT purposes at the open market value. But the situation that gives rise to that power is only where a "taxable person" is the supplier. Thus, the person must already be registerable or registered for that to be the case. As such, this power does not apply to a person if that person is correctly unregistered on the basis of the value chosen for the supply. Note, however, that this is no cover for "barter" which is always counted towards registration.

4. Cases where supplies can appear to be hidden

4.1 Introduction

There are several situations where money, or some kind of benefit in kind, is allowed to transfer between entities, but where it may not be clear whether the payment or benefit is consideration which is relevant to the VAT registration requirement, rather than being no more than a movement of value between entities. Several such situations are considered below, in an attempt to warn readers of possible cases of contention.

4.2 Supply of staff

Where an entity allows another entity (including a wholly owned subsidiary, or other closely related entity) to use its own staff there is a danger that this will give rise to taxable supplies of staff, or supplies of the services underlying the use of staff (for example IT or HR services). The biggest danger is that people often assume that the staff are jointly employed where more than one legal entity makes up a closely knit inter-dependent group of organisations. They will thus "share" staff costs. They may often fail to raise specific charges on invoices for doing so, but rather operate an inter-company account in which the staff costs are effectively shared. This may not come to light even through the statutory accounts, which may simply partition the staff costs directly to each set of accounts, without showing an amount being charged by one to the other.

Where there are bulletproof joint contracts of employment between these entities, this may well be satisfactory, since the party that operates the payroll and pays the salaries to the staff could be regarded as acting as an agent, in part, for the other entities. But where there is one legal employer, it is not possible to infer a joint employment situation. In that case, supplies are made between the entities, at least in most situations.

This gives rise to one of the most common reasons for failing to register for VAT where exempt service providers, in particular, are concerned. For instance, businesses in the finance sector, the education sector, the health sector, and similar exempt sectors, will commonly form special purpose vehicle entities, but then treat them as though they were simply divisions of a single entity. If the employment contract stays with just one entity (probably the holding company) and the costs are shared, then this gives rise to supplies.

Even though employee remuneration is specifically excluded from the scope of VAT by the *Principal VAT Directive* where a payment is made to an employee, a further sharing of employment costs is consideration for a supply which will generally be within the scope of VAT, and taxable. The following, however, are concessionary treatments which may override this, though the position needs to be considered in some detail:

1. Where two non-profit bodies second staff that work on non-business activities, and make charges merely to cover the costs.

2. Where the entire responsibility for paying the salary and related taxes, to and for the member of staff who is seconded from one company to another, is passed to the recipient company. But this only applies where, in addition, the seconding company receives absolutely no financial reward, whether monetarily or in kind, by virtue of the secondment. Note that this does not work for shared staff, but only for proper secondments.

3. Where a company can impose a director upon another company (such as a subsidiary company), and simply recoups the cost of paying the director.

It is worth making a passing mention of the provisions of VATA 1994, Sch. 9, Group 16, relating to exemption from VAT for "cost-sharing". This is not strictly to do with registration, but it is relevant to the problem of staff sharing. It allows for an exemption to apply to sharing of services (including staff time) but only subject to extremely difficult conditions. It is worth reviewing these as an alternative approach to reducing VAT burdens on staff sharing.

Law: EC/2006/112

4.3 Compensation

Compensation is treated as a payment that:

- is not in return for a supply;
- is therefore not consideration; and
- is thus outside the scope of VAT.

But the difficulty is to understand what is really meant by "compensation". This difficulty is exacerbated by the fact that the phrase is commonly used in a rather loose way to denote reciprocation for services rendered, particularly where employees are concerned. This can give a view that an over-liberal interpretation of "compensation" will avoid the need to charge VAT. In fact, VAT requires one to define compensation in a more narrow way, and the following general points act as a guide.

Compensation arises where an entity:

- has infringed another's rights without its permission, or
- has shouldered the explicit burden of providing compensation in certain eventualities.

The first instance could involve an entity which in effect trespasses on another's territory (say for example, where there is an exclusive right to sell a product in a country, but another party illegally fails to observe this, or where copyright is infringed). The payment will not be for an agreed provision of a right or other services, but rather will be to compensate for an infringement that was not agreed. Accordingly, the aggrieved party cannot be said to have provided any service to the party which damaged it. In such situations this will be a genuine form of compensation, and thus outside the scope of VAT.

In the second situation, we have cases that are typically covered by insurance companies, but may also arise in any case of indemnity or surety. The insurance company will agree to bear the burden of paying some of the money, or providing restitution of goods, in return for a premium for shifting the risk. The insurance payout is no more than compensation, and is not for selling goods or services by the insured to the insurer. That is the case even though there may be a subrogation clause which allows the insurer to take ownership of damaged goods etc. This is merely regarded as a

51

related protection to the insurer, and is not regarded as the making of a supply by the insured to the insurer.

Example

Shields Ltd receives two different and unconnected payments. One is from Dodds Ltd because Dodds Ltd breached a patent held by Shields Ltd and was ordered by a court to pay damages to Shields Ltd. Shields Ltd also suffered vandalism to a complex piece of machinery and made an insurance claim. The insurer took title to the vandalised machinery and then paid the negotiated payment under the insurance contract.

The payment from Dodds Ltd did not involve Shields Ltd agreeing to give up rights to the patent to Dodds Ltd, but rather was received to compensate it for Dodds Ltd's illegal actions. The payment is thus outside the scope of VAT. The insurance payment was not consideration for transferring title to the machinery to the insurer, but compensation for the damage sustained.

Shields Ltd then receives a further payment from Goodman Ltd in respect of sales Shields Ltd made to Goodman Ltd but where a commercial dispute relating to those goods arose. Goodman Ltd and Shields Ltd settle on half price being paid and the goods being retained by Goodman Ltd. In this case, though there was a dispute, the payment is clearly "for" the goods, and thus the payment is not compensation, but is consideration for the supply.

Property related examples

There can be disputes over situations where amounts are paid before there has been an infringement, but in circumstances where it is clear that an infringement is more or less inevitable. It can be a debatable point as to whether that means that the payment is compensation, since it would be inevitable that the infringement would occur, or whether in effect the parties had agreed a bargain, and that this meant that a right had been sold.

A classic example of that, in the writer's experience, is "compensation" for infringing another party's right to light. Such payments are almost always regarded as compensation, and HMRC tend to accept that they are outside the scope of VAT. But, usually, the agreement for compensation is reached prior to the right being infringed and in effect in return for the damaged party to withdraw their opposition and to pave the way for a resolution. It is interesting that HMRC do not take a more aggressive line on this (and there does appear to be an inconsistency with the SDLT treatment).

HMRC also appear to think that where a payment is due under a lease in return for a landlord agreeing to do something, and where the lease allows that thing to be done, but as long as the "compensation" is paid, then that can be regarded as genuine compensation rather than buying a right. The reasoning behind this is that the right is already inherent in the lease, although it has to be paid for by way of the compensation in question. That seems hardly convincing, but it is HMRC policy at the time of writing.

Interest charged on late rent is also usually regarded as compensation rather than further rent. Car parking fines for infringement are regarded as compensation rather than an extra charge for extra car parking supplies (though not deliberate overpayment).

The CJEU has held (in *Trinity Mirror*) that a payment made to a new tenant for agreeing to take the grant of a lease is not consideration for a supply unless he is an anchor tenant or agrees to carry out some specific activity (such as landlord's works). Thus it is deemed to be some kind of "cash back" deal rather than a transaction. Curiously, this is not regarded as the case where the assignment of an existing lease is concerned, which is regarded as creating a taxable supply by the assignee of agreeing to accept the lease (see *Cantor Fitzgerald*). The reasons for this distinction are obscure to say the least.

Where hotels are concerned, a payment to reserve a bed for the night, but where the booking is not taken up, is regarded as turning into compensation at the point of the "no show" as long as the reservation was not for a particular room, but only for one of the rooms. Any amount retained from the deposit is treated as compensation because no particular supply was made.

"Breakage deposits" are generally treated as advance compensation and not a taxable supply at the time they are taken.

It can be seen that determining the difference between genuine compensation and consideration for a supply is not an easy point.

Cases: *C&E Commrs v Cantor Fitzgerald International* C-108/99, [2011] STC 1453; *Trinity Mirror plc (formerly Mirror Group Newspapers Ltd) v C&E Commrs* C-409/96

Agreeing to refrain

It may be tempting to think that any payment made to a party for their agreeing not to do something (such as not to compete in a certain area) has to be a form of compensation since not doing something cannot be a service. This is wrong. Agreeing not to do something, or to refrain, is in fact a service, and payment would be consideration and thus within the scope of VAT.

4.4 Management services

A subject which is very closely aligned with supplies of staff is the supply of underlying services such as administration or management services. The distinction between the two is mainly that a management service will include not merely the human resource, but also other technical resources.

Management services are taxable supplies and count towards VAT registration. However, situations can arise where there may be some doubt as to whether there has been a management service or whether, conversely, payments are made which could be regarded as falling short of such a service.

The case of surrendering group relief between related companies is usually cited as the classic example where there is not necessarily any supply of services. A company in a corporate group may incur a tax loss and surrender it to another company in the group. A company may claim group relief and surrender all or part of that payment to another company in the group. Following the precedent set in an early VAT tribunal case *Tilling Management Services*, these payments are not regarded as consideration at all, but merely the transfer of value between companies. That said, this assumes that no actual management services are provided. If, on the other hand, management services are provided without consideration, except that the company being managed is required to surrender a loss, or a group relief payment, then that would be different. The payment may very well represent the value of the services. On the whole it would be advisable for companies not to express the right to the transfer of a loss or group relief payment as being in consideration of anything at all. Where a "nexus" can be established between the two, then it does appear to be a supply of services which can count towards VAT registration.

Case: *Tilling Management Services* [1979] STC 365

Impact on dividend

Where a holding company provides management input into its subsidiaries, but does not set any charge for this, the services provided are not regarded as services for VAT purposes because no consideration passes. Services are treated as not being a supply at all if there is no consideration for them.

The obvious corollary appears to be that the profit made by the subsidiary companies will increase, not having to bear a management cost, and that this will create a greater distributable profit by way of dividend to the holding company. A dividend itself is regarded as outside the scope of VAT as a form of profit distribution. The question that arises is whether, without having raised the charge for the management services provided, any part of the dividend can be regarded as consideration for the management services.

On the whole that should not be the case, even though it does appear arguable that it might be so in extreme circumstances. It may thus be beneficial, if the subsidiary companies carry out exempt activities, for the holding company not to charge for management services, but rather to take an increased dividend. But HMRC could decide to challenge this by reference to a rule relating to delays in making charges for management services (discussed below). But if there is any linkage between dividends paid and management services provided (which would be unusual), this would encourage HMRC to take the view that consideration is passing and that there are taxable supplies which could be caught by VAT registration.

4.5 Phoney management services

Where holding companies make charges to subsidiaries it cannot be assumed that this means that supplies are definitely being made. If there is no substance to the arrangement, HMRC will usually treat the sums as mere movements of finance and not consideration for any supply (although it would be unwise to rely on that to avoid what might be a compulsory registration liability). Where a holding company imposes a director on a subsidiary and receives reimbursement of the director's salary from the subsidiary, this is not regarded as the making of a supply since the situation was not consensual.

4.6 Delayed consideration between related companies

As mentioned above, the "free supply of services" is not regarded as a supply for VAT purposes. However, where the intention is for a charge to be made (either in money or in kind), but that charge is delayed, HMRC perceive the possibility of unacceptable avoidance. Accordingly, regulations have been laid to counteract this by deeming the time of supply to occur at an earlier stage than payment (reg. 94B of the *VAT Regulations* 1995).

The circumstances in which this would apply generally are as follows:

- services which are normally regarded as continuous services (in which general management services would be included) are supplied by a service company within the corporate group;
- one or more of the members of the corporate group to which the supplies are made is unable to reclaim all VAT incurred; and
- the services are generically taxable at a positive rate.

Where payment is not regularly made for the services, the tax point for the services is deemed to be 12 months after the supplies commenced. There is nothing that requires the supplier to be already VAT registered for this rule to apply. Therefore, if a non-VAT registered supplier of services in these circumstances carries out the activity for more than 12 months without drawing up an account, an automatic tax point could cause it to be registered for VAT with effect from that particular date, probably based around the "look forward" test where the supplies exceed the threshold.

This is difficult enough to deal with, but bizarrely there is a further rule to the effect that this particular tax point can then be ignored if payment is made within six months after that date. Thus, if the business is aware that it will receive payment within six months of the 12-month point, it need not register for VAT at the 12 month point, because it will then register with effect from the payment date (again, subject to the registration value thresholds). However, if it does not fulfil that intention, the time of supply naturally defaults back to the 12-month date. Or, at least, that is one interpretation of the rules. On the contrary, it could be argued that the original tax point set at 12 months is correct until it is literally replaced by the date of payment and that the VAT registration obligation set at 12 months could not be displaced merely by a later event. Had the legislation been considered more carefully this kind of conundrum might have been avoided.

This set of provisions does not deem there to be consideration where none exists, but rather deems there to be a tax point where the consideration (and thus tax point) is delayed to the extent provided.

Excludes "free supplies"

As if to make matters even more difficult, there is nothing in this legislation which states that a "free supply of services" is caught by it. This does not deem there to be consideration where none exists, but rather deems there to be a tax point where the consideration (and thus tax point) is delayed to the extent provided. Thus, if a company is to give services deliberately for no consideration, this rule does not appear to apply, although one can expect HMRC to argue that it does. Only if there is a view to a charge being made does the deemed tax point appear to be relevant. This leads to the question of how one might evidence an intention to make a charge in such circumstances. This takes us on to the question of intercompany debts.

Law: SI 1995/2518, reg. 94B

4.7 Intercompany debts

In the above example, we postulated the possibility that a company providing management services would not intend to charge. Where that is the case, it cannot therefore accrue a value of potential charge to the other company, since that would mean it did intend to charge. Accordingly, any internal management accounting which purports to show that there is a potential charge between the two companies, acts as some kind of "smoking gun" in respect of the application of reg. 94B. One would probably have to assume, then, that the deemed tax point arrangements do actually apply.

However, simply entering accrued liabilities in the management accounts does not count as actual payment. In accordance with an old case, *Pentex Oil*, indebtedness has to be paid off in order to give rise to consideration. Thus the entering of a debt in internal management accounts does not create consideration between the parties. Nor, in fact, does entering a liability on the balance sheet of statutory accounts between companies. All these do is show that an amount is to be paid, but has not yet been paid. If the services are such that they only set a tax point when they are paid for, then the tax point has not yet arrived.

But, on the contrary, if (say) Kell Ltd owes an amount to Fell Ltd, and, later, Fell Ltd owes an amount to Kell Ltd, and the two are matched off in the intercompany accounts, then clearly Kell Ltd's indebtedness to Fell Ltd is reduced, thus connoting consideration passing. Thus, the set off of one debt against the other does constitute consideration. It is only where debt is shown from one side alone that there is no payment. This is therefore a significant trap for the unwary.

It is also often commented that where payment is shown as arising in the statutory accounts, it does not matter whether there has been an actual transfer of cash from one bank account to another, and it is enough on its own to set the tax point as at the date of signing the accounts. This is true only up to a point. If the statutory accounts show an amount having been charged, but no balance sheet entry for the payment yet to be made, then on the surface of it, the payment has been made. Whether that is correct accounting is another matter.

The *Mark Reid* case also established that, where several companies have yet to pay fees to a person or company, and those companies, being related, allow the liability to be consolidated into the intercompany account between only one of their number and supplier (with, perhaps, separate intercompany account liabilities being set up between the associated companies), these movements of liability are treated as little more than "housekeeping" and do not connote the payment of consideration. That said, they will undoubtedly cause HMRC to believe that there has been consideration where they see sums being moved between accounts, albeit without a comparable bank entry.

Where groups of companies work in a largely VAT exempt area such that they are not VAT registered, it is extremely easy for the accounting between the parties to give the impression, if no more than that, of consideration passing for joint procurement of services. Sometimes this is real (in which case there is a literal problem with VAT registration for the services) and sometimes it is illusory (in which case the problem is also illusory). The important thing to ensure is that transactions do not appear to be entered into, and are not actually entered into, which could trigger VAT registration without considering the VAT connotations.

Cases: *Pentex Oil* EDN/91/140; *Mark Reid (Reid & Co)* [2013] UKFTT 241 TC

4.8 Disbursements

The question of how to tax disbursements usually arises in the context of VAT registered participants, so it is dealt with only briefly here.

A true disbursement is an action by a service provider in procuring a service which is then provided directly by a third party to his client, and then dealing with the banking arrangements by passing the cash to the third party supplier. Sometimes disbursements relate to statutory charges rather than supplies. In either case the VAT analysis is the same. The party that makes the disbursement is not making a supply by virtue of the underlying activity. It is merely passing money backwards and forwards. Thus, the value of VAT disbursement does not form part of his taxable supplies.

But expense reimbursements are quite different. These are often called disbursements when they are not. A classic example of a true disbursement would be where solicitors charge land registry fees to clients (though not search fees, following the decision in the case of *Brabners*). A classic example of a reimbursed expense which falls within the value of the service is the addition of travelling costs to

59

an invoice where the travelling was undertaken by the supplier to enable him to carry out a supply.

Consequently, it can be very important to determine where there is a specific disbursement (outside the scope of VAT) and where there is an expense reimbursement (which could well be taxable). The underlying theory behind this is that where an expense is a necessary outlay by the service provider in order to enable him to provide his service, then it will be part of his turnover (and have similar connotations to the debate discussed elsewhere in this book concerning agent/principal). But where it is merely the passing of money to a third party, then that does not form part of the service of the entity which carries out the monetary transfer.

So, it is important to understand what criteria are generally applied to define a disbursement in the true sense. These are:

- that the third party supply was not a necessary adjunct of supplies by the entity making the disbursement;
- that the third party was contracted directly with the final consumer, even though the party making the disbursement may have made all of the practical arrangements;
- that in law it is possible for the third party to approach the customer to pay the disbursement, such that the entity making the disbursement is merely doing so for convenience;
- that the disbursement is a separate figure on a statement of account or invoice, and is the exact figure charged;
- that both the final customer and the provider of the service (or, as appropriate, the levying authority) are thus aware of each other's identity and therefore are not "blind" to the fact that supplies are being made to each other; and
- finally, it should not be possible for the party making the disbursement to change the value of the disbursement, to discount it, or to increase it, since this strongly implies that it is not a mere disbursement. Thus, the exact amount charged by the third party has to be paid to it, and obtained from the final customer; no more no less.

Case: *Brabners LLP v HMRC* [2017] UKFTT 666 TC

4.9 Hotels

Although likely to be of extremely limited relevance, it is worth noting that a room letting to an occupant who has stayed more than four weeks is regarded as being at a value lower than the payment he makes. It can be as little as 20% of that payment though that depends on the cost of the services provided to him. This can have the unexpected effect of creating a higher effective threshold for such hotels.

Law: VATA 1994, Sch. 6, para. 9

5. Whether a business

5.1 "Business" and "economic activity"

Irrespective of the basis upon which VAT registration arises, it will only arise in regard to activity which is "in the course or furtherance of a business". In plain terms, transactions in return for payment are not within the scope of VAT at all (and are therefore not a "taxable supply") unless the activity amounts to a "business".

The EU VAT legislation on this does not use the word "business", but rather the even vaguer concept of "economic activity". However, there should be no difference in the interpretation between these two terminologies. That said, the likelihood at the time of writing that the UK will exit the EU rather changes this situation, although any divergence between the interpretation of the two terminologies is likely to prove to be a slow process. The remainder of this chapter focuses only on the current rules prior to Brexit.

Difficulty often arises when language is used within the EU in a way which is not on all fours with the UK use of language. For instance, the Court of Justice of the European Union (CJEU) has in the past referred to an entity's "business" as really meaning its "activities", or what it exists to do, without trying to suggest that this is within the scope of "economic activity". Thus, what it would call "business" could amount to what under UK legislation would be regarded as "non-business".

This terminological clash extends to the definition of "taxable person". In the UK, a person is regarded as a taxable person if he is registered for VAT or if he ought to be (even though he is not). In EU terminology, a taxable person is any party which carries out an economic activity whether or not it has reached the point where it should be registered for VAT. These significant differences in meaning are unfortunate and appear to have arisen owing to the misguided notion that by translating "Eurospeak" into "plain English" one would have fewer rather than more difficulties. That is not the case.

Mining, exploitation of property, and membership of clubs, are deemed specifically in the Directive to be business activities.

Law: VATA 1994, s. 3(1), 4; EC/2006/112, art. 9

5.2 Recognising a business

5.2.1 *Introduction*

There are many strands to this issue which are explored below.

As a general principle, a business transaction will only arise where the parties can exercise some degree of autonomy in accepting (or declining) the opportunity to make or receive the supply. Where there is literal compulsion to do so in any given scenario, then it is unlikely that the interaction between the parties amounts to a business interaction. (See the point made above about the imposition of directors on subsidiary company boards by holding companies.)

The nature of the discretion that can be exercised does not, however, relate to whether or not one entity is in need of doing something. An entity can have no choice as regards that need, but nonetheless decides how to meet it, and that would (possibly) involve a business interaction. It is only if he has no discretion in the matter that there is no supply. The most obvious example is where an entity is required to pay tax or a "levy". Whilst something good may come of that payment, it was not a consensual situation, so the payment is not consideration for a supply (*Apple and Pear Development Council*).

Equally, where a person decides to make a payment even though he would have received the perceived benefit whether or not he had made the payment, then the payment is not "for" the benefit, and there is no transaction. This is simply a gift, even though it was occasioned by a feeling on the part of the giver that he had benefited and perhaps ought to reciprocate (*Tolsma*). The clearest example of this is the street musician. He collects donations from passers by. These are not consideration for a supply even though the people making payment have benefited from the music. They would have benefited whether or not they paid, so the payment could not be "for" the supply.

Cases: *Apple and Pear Development Council v C & E Commrs* C-102/86, [1988] STC 221; *Tolsma v Inspecteur der Omzetbelasting Leeuwarden* C-16/93; [1994] STC 509

5.2.2 Whether private activities

It is important to understand that sales in return for consideration can be carried out by private people in a manner which does not connote a natural business. For instance, a private individual may decide to sell his car when purchasing another, but will not be selling his car in the course or furtherance of a business by him, but rather is merely disposing of his own private assets. However, this might not be true if the private individual bought cars with a view to selling them in reasonably rapid succession, and happened to drive them while they were on hand. It certainly would not be true if he bought several cars, only driving (say) one of them, and immediately sought customers for the others. On the other hand, a vintage car collector, for instance, might wish to buy several cars and keep them for private enjoyment, but will from time to time dispose of cars with which he is no longer in love. Thus it may be obvious where private individuals are simply disposing of their private assets, but it is not always obvious where the line is crossed between such behaviour and an emergent business activity.

Hobby business

There is also the issue of the "hobby business". A person may decide to manufacture wooden bowls on a lathe. He does so rather more for hobby than commercial reasons. Nonetheless, he wishes to sell the output, and will often sell to friends and relatives, or perhaps at local school/church fairs. The intelligent bystander might well take the view that this does not amount to a business, since it is just a hobby which happens to involve some sales along the way as a collateral by-product. But that is hardly clear, and may particularly become challengeable if he decides to start selling his wares at, say, car boot sales, or on internet auction sites, or if he takes his products around summer fairs in his general locality.

It has to be admitted that, in both of the above kinds of example, they are usually saved from determining the point by the fact that compulsory VAT registration in any case only arises once the turnover from this business exceeds a significant figure. Indeed, it is certainly possible to run a true business on a smaller scale than the VAT registration thresholds, and for an individual to earn a decent living through such a business. But there may be some unusual cases where the value of the sales does exceed the thresholds, and then the point arises as to whether it is a business, in order to determine whether the supplier should register for VAT. Examples where this may be the case are:

- original works of art from an aspirant painter who is not yet fully established as such;
- sales of works of art by a family that has the resources to buy and sell on some scale;
- an amateur author who could receive royalties above the thresholds, but embarked upon the activity purely as a hobby which then became more successful than perhaps expected.

No doubt there are other possible scenarios where this might be true.

It is also worth noting that, unless the activity is classed as a business, the supplier is not permitted to register voluntarily for VAT (regarding which see **Chapter 9**), and HMRC have a record of alleging a lack of a business to counter such applications.

Rule of thumb

This means that we need some kind of "rule of thumb" to determine the hallmarks of a business activity as distinct from a non-business activity.

The interpretation of such a "rule" has been impacted by the Court of Appeal decision in *Longridge*. This 2016 decision casts considerable doubt on traditional tests discussed below. The decision says that these tests may continue to play a role, but it left a doubt as to what that role might be, or when they should be applied. Instead, it substituted a test from the CJEU decision in *Republic of Finland*, to the effect that any permanent activity which involves making supplies for consideration is a business.

Whether a business

At the time of writing, HMRC have yet to comment on how they will apply this decision. However, they have continued to use the older interpretations where small businesses are concerned, particularly in dealing with the borderline between personal enthusiasms and potential business operations. This may suggest that they will apply the *Longridge* test to larger enterprises. This, however, leaves uncertainty as to where that borderline is. At the moment, we can only assume that most scenarios will be covered by the new interpretation. More is said about this in **5.2.3** in regard to the impact on charities.

The precedent of *Lord Fisher* continues to apply to smaller operations (arguably). Its principles are that a business will arise where a decent proportion of the following are present (as dependent on the nature of the business of course):

1. it is "a serious undertaking earnestly pursued";
2. it is of sufficient scale and (as relevant) regularity to constitute a business;
3. it is of sufficient financial substance;
4. it is run on sound business lines;
5. it is an activity identical or similar to that which would be carried out by others as a business;
6. it is "principally concerned with the making of taxable supplies".

Some of these provisions are not particularly easy to interpret. It is possible to follow a hobby as a serious undertaking earnestly pursued, although admittedly that would very rarely apply to the mere disposal of one's private assets. Having sufficient scale and regularity rather begs the question as to what is sufficient (though insufficient scale to breach the turnover thresholds decides that point automatically unless one is interested in pursuing voluntary registration). Anything above the VAT registration thresholds must surely be regarded as having sufficient scale in itself, though that alone will not determine that it is a business.

But regularity (or perhaps frequency) is a rather different point. If one only sporadically enters into the activity, or does so as a "one off", then perhaps it is not really a business in any recognised sense.

Running the operation on sound and efficient business lines appears to be a reasonably objective test. Of course, an organisation cannot avoid VAT registration simply by saying that they are rather poorly run, and are, in effect, an incompetent operation. But, giving no real care and attention to the operational underpinnings of a business may be regarded as indicative of an activity which was intended to be entirely private and would have no application to the wider public.

A critical point, in the writer's view, is whether the activity is in competition with identical or similar activities or, to put it more accurately, whether it is an activity of a kind that people in business would undertake as their business. There seems to be an obvious point here, that an activity which no business in its rightful mind would undertake could not normally be regarded as a business at all. However, this test only operates in one direction, namely to exclude activities of reasonable scale. It does not prove that an activity is a business simply because it appears to be similar to what a business would undertake. For instance, the hobby business (such as making wooden bowls) could very easily be run as a business by someone else, but may fail to be a business on the basis of failing the other tests mentioned here. If a private individual sells his old washing machine for scrap, it would not be argued, surely, that he was competing with recycling businesses. Therefore, this has limited application, but otherwise is a somewhat key test.

The most difficult of all of these to comprehend is the test of whether the activity is predominantly concerned with the making of [taxable] supplies. Indeed, this is the test that was most criticised in the *Longridge* decision, and must now be regarded as almost redundant. However, for the record, if only historical, the following comments help to analyse its application.

First, a business can be concerned with making exempt supplies, so to that extent the test has been wrongly formulated from the start. But if one strips out the otiose reference to "taxable", one is left with a test which is extremely difficult to apply. How can one determine whether there is a principal concern in making supplies as distinct from carrying out the activity itself? Should the mere fact that a person decided to undertake the activity in order to create the deliverable outcome (perhaps services relating to care and welfare, or the production of wooden bowls for their artistic merit) and therefore merely sells the services or goods in order to cover the costs, really mean that they are not in business, when another party wishes to enter into it with a view to profit and thus is a business? If that was the case, then surely one of the criteria of whether there is a business activity is whether there is an intention to make profit. But that is not the case.

Indeed, a major contrast between the VAT principles of what constitutes a business, and the direct tax "badges of trade", is that any view to making a profit is irrelevant to whether there is a business activity. This is clear from all EU jurisprudence on the matter. It is possible to run a business on a structurally non-profit making basis. Charities, for instance, can run businesses on precisely that basis. The criterion of either making a profit, or seeking to do so, is entirely absent from the tests. Thus it is not possible to interpolate into the test some kind of profit motive. But, where does that leave us? How do we determine what the principal objective of the supplier is? What is it that determines that his objective was making supplies, as distinct from simply creating the outcomes that those supplies support?

It is worth noting that HMRC have tripped up over these tests in the cases of *de Ferranti* and *Gravel Road Records,* where they wrongly used these tests to attempt to deny VAT registration.

We are left with a highly impressionistic tool where, taking all things together, we have to arrive at a general view by "standing back" and looking at the entire picture. This is hardly a satisfactory position to be in. It essentially brings us back to the first point that has been raised. If the turnover in question exceeds the VAT registration thresholds, and assuming of course that it does not involve the sale of capital assets (which as mentioned elsewhere are excluded from the turnover tally), then there ought to be a presumption that a business is going on and that VAT registration may be mandatory. It is only where there is a complete lack of regularity in the activity, or where the supply in question is the sale of a high value asset which has not been linked to any ongoing business, that it will possibly be safe to assume that there is no business activity.

Before any adviser, or person, decides to take the view that, notwithstanding exceeding the thresholds, their activity is not a business and therefore not covered by VAT registration, they will need to look in depth at the various precedents on this to determine where their particular circumstances lie.

Cases: *C&E Commrs v Lord Fisher* [1981] STC 238; *Republic of Finland* (2009) C-246/08; *de Ferranti v HMRC* [2011] UKFTT 435 (TC); *Longridge on the Thames* [2016] EWCA Civ 930; *Gravel Road Records Ltd v HMRC* [2017] UKFTT 80 (TC).

5.2.3 Charities and non-business activities

Typical examples

This subject is far removed from the issue of micro-businesses, hobby businesses, and disposing of private assets. Charities are often very small, but those charities that are involved in making supplies in return for consideration are often the larger ones, and would tend to be serious undertakings which are earnestly pursued and run according to sound business principles. Nonetheless, charities often tend to be involved in non-business activities by virtue of certain other factors.

A good deal of the case law relating to what is or is not a business arises from charity case law. However, the paradox here is that this often derives from a desire by charities to qualify for certain VAT reliefs on expenditure which only apply where it does not carry out a business activity, rather than to determine whether or not a charity should register for VAT. This is because a large proportion of what charities do in return for payment is in fact exempt from VAT rather than taxable in the first place. Thus, the distinction between an activity which does not amount to a business, and an activity which, whilst being a business, is the making of exempt supplies, appears to be irrelevant to the subject of VAT registration.

On rare occasions it could have that impact since exemptions have to be applied in strict terms, and there may be scenarios where the services in question, whilst being wholly charitable in nature, do not qualify for exemption, and therefore could cause a charity to need to register for VAT and charge it if it cannot argue that it is carrying out a non-business activity.

The following points apply to non-profit entities, not all of which are charities, but which we will refer to as charities for convenience.

The following activities by a charity will often be regarded as being non-business:

1. Income arising from investments (although these would otherwise be exempt).
2. Where the activity is funded by the charity's resources or external "grants" or "donations", since neither grants nor donations are charges, and therefore the activity does not involve transactions.
3. Cases where charges are sometimes made but on a somewhat sporadic basis, and not with any consistent attempt to make supplies in return for consideration (such as where a service is provided mostly free of charge, but a certain class of recipient is regarded as being able to afford the service and is therefore asked to pay for it – see *Finland*).
4. Where charges are always made (or almost always made), but the terms on which they are made are so adverse that it could be regarded that the activity is not a business in any case. For the most part these activities will be exempt if they were not non-business, but they could from time to time even be taxable.

Case: *CEC v Republic of Finland* C-246/08

Grants and donations

A true grant or donation is a payment made in prospect of receiving nothing in return. Thus, the payment is not consideration for any supply. If the activity carried out by a charity is supported solely by grants and donations, then it will not be a business activity, and there will not be a value of taxable supplies for the purposes of VAT registration.

Whilst this all sounds very simple, there are some distinct problems with it:

1. Ostensible grants or donations could be consideration if the donor is provided with certain benefits, even if they are intended to be something of a "token" or acknowledgement, since then something is given in consideration of the payment. For business, this could be exposure of its corporate logo, or the provision of an

intellectual property right. For an individual, this could be access to meetings or certain kinds of entertainment.

2. Where something is given in return for the payment, then one cannot simply assume that the payment is a mixture of donation and of consideration for the value of the benefits given in return. It is established case law (*Tron Theatre*) that the entire payment then becomes the value of the supply, except in circumstances where all of the benefits provided in return have an objective market value which makes them readily available on the "high street", thus effectively fixing a value. Thus there is a real danger that even an excessive amount of money in relation to the benefits provided would all be regarded as consideration, which, if taxable, all goes towards the registration thresholds.

3. The same treatment almost always arises in cases of "commercial participation". This is where, say, a manufacturer promises, as part of a contractual arrangement between the charity and itself, that it will provide a certain payment per unit sold of its product in return for the charity allowing the supplier to claim that it will make such a donation when marketing its goods to potential customers. This is regarded for VAT purposes as the charity providing a promotional or marketing service to the manufacturer/supplier of the product, and the "donation" paid for this is then treated as consideration for that promotional service.

4. By extension, where a commercial supplier sells goods or services on the footing that part of the price is a donation to a charity, that donative element is not subtracted from the price. The full price is relevant for VAT registration purposes.

5. Funding agreements often require that the grantor shall receive intellectual property rights. This is not harmful if the sole purpose of the clause is to allow the grantor to publish the results of any particular activity (for example research) to the widest possible audience for no further charge. However, if it can be shown that the payer received information that was essentially private

and could be of commercial advantage to it, this could well be regarded as payment for a benefit and thus the payment becomes consideration for a supply of intellectual property which will often be a taxable supply.

6. Whilst the above are general "rules of thumb", the following exceptions generally also apply. Where the logo of a funding body such as the Lottery Heritage Fund, or a government department, is shown, this is not normally treated as commercial advertising, and therefore the grant remains a true grant. Certain things that could be regarded as benefits are often regarded otherwise, such as general information about the activities of the charity, "naming rights" to such things as a building, the wing of a building, or a function within a venue, and any bare acknowledgement of generosity such as given in an annual report, theatre programmes and plaques in buildings.

Where the above points are at issue, it is usually possible for separate agreements to be entered into for the benefits, for a particular fixed price, and for the balance to be a donation or grant, and thus outside the scope of VAT. However, considerable care has to be exercised in entering into such arrangements to avoid implicitly linking the two together and causing the donation element to be, in substance and reality, consideration for the services in question. In particular, it must be possible for the grantor/donor to demand to receive the benefits for the fixed benefit price without making the actual donation itself. This is not usually problematic where the grantor/donor is properly motivated to give the donation, but on the margins it may cause certain people and companies to seek to take advantage of the situation.

Special care should be taken in arranging for a split between a contractual sum and a donative element. Where the charity is not registered for VAT, the value of the contractual sum could be critical if the supplies are taxable. Whilst it may be tempting to ensure that the value set allows the charity not to have to register for VAT, if the value is set at an implausibly low level, such as for example to be below the cost of providing the benefits, HMRC may seek to attack the entire arrangement on the basis that the charity could not legally have sold the benefits at a loss without some degree of certainty in receiving the grants or donations. Whilst the charity law point on that is far from resoundingly in support of HMRC's potential argument, and HMRC are therefore ambivalent about launching this argument, it should be borne in mind that an artificial valuation is likely to cause HMRC to look for weaknesses in the arrangements.

Case: *C&E Commrs v Tron Theatre Ltd* [1994] STC 177

Grant or subsidy?

A further threat lies in wait for situations where it seems plain that the grant-giving body receives no benefit at all, and the activity is purely for the public benefit.

In such a case it would seem, on the surface, that there can be no taxable supply for consideration. But this will not be the case if the grant is deemed to be a "subsidy". Subsidies are deemed to be part of the consideration for a service provided. Confusingly, it is possible for the subsidy to be the entirety of the consideration for the service provided. Therefore if a donor supports specific provision of services by the charity to any other party or parties, so as to allow that party to pay less than what would otherwise have been the economic charge (or perhaps nothing at all) for the service, then it is possible for HMRC to argue that the grant is in fact a subsidy and therefore there is a taxable supply to the third party recipient of the services. Under this arrangement, the grantor is regarded as simply paying the bills of the third party, rather than providing a grant towards general provision of services to the community as a whole.

Again we have a situation here where there is no clear dividing line. The principal cases on which this notion is based relate, on the one hand, to subsidies for publications where it was held that the subsidy was linked so directly to the provision of these publications for no further charge, that it was in fact a charge for the publications. The other case concerned grants drawn down by a consultancy company which provided advice to householders as to how to insulate their houses. As there was a clear product which had a particular agreed tariff (albeit paid by the grant-making body), it was decided that there was a taxable supply to the beneficiaries of the service, albeit paid for out of a pot of money that happened to be described as a "grant". This kind of consultancy would normally be taxable, so the example is relevant to our discussions.

So, how does one know when one has crossed the line from a true grant into a "subsidy"? Unfortunately this is extremely difficult territory. As a result of the *Groundworks Cheshire* VAT tribunal case, the position has become very unclear. In that case, the benefit to the recipient of the services did not involve particular units of identical activity, but rather a bespoke service for which the grants paid up to a finite amount, and this was found to be a case of making taxable supplies.

Case: *Groundworks Cheshire* [2012] UKFTT 750 (TC)

Grants where service is provided

It is also not uncommon to find that ostensible grants are in fact consideration for services provided to the payer. This tends to arise where the payer is a local authority, an agency (quango) set up by government for a specific purpose, or a central government department which has a particular agenda of its own to follow. If, all things considered, the payer is deriving a specific benefit from the services which it needs to procure for itself, then the payment is consideration for those services. Again, the question of where the line is crossed between funding of a charity's own activities (non-business) and procuring services for the payer (business and potentially taxable) is so vague as to be almost imperceptible, and is a highly subjective area. The best that can be done is to put forward the following points, which are often adopted by auditors to determine whether income is earned contractual income, or is potentially a restricted fund grant.

It is convenient to formulate the guidance by seeking to define where a service provision is likely to have arisen, since in that case, there is a danger of VAT registration being applicable.

These indicia are that:

1. The specification for the services in question came from the funder rather than being originated by the charity (as that suggests that the funder wanted something performed for him).

2. The funder receives a "product", such as the outcome of commissioned research, or rights to use the services produced on a preferential or exclusive basis. For instance, a local authority could ask for a charity to carry out satisfaction tests of school leavers in its area, and provide it with the resulting data.

3. The funder has a statutory obligation to carry out the activity, and therefore in effect must procure its performance (outsourcing).

4. The funder is the sole payer for the service (since if it shared the funding burden at all broadly with other funders, it would be inherently unlikely that it was receiving services that another participant was funding on its behalf).

5. The services or goods that are deliverable under the arrangement are very specifically outlined in such a fashion that it would be possible to enforce the contract and recognise where it had not been performed properly. An example would be, say, the provision of 100 legal counselling sessions to needy people in a particular area, where it is clear whether or not the 100 sessions have actually been performed, and it is unlikely that more than 100 will be performed without further payment. However, this would probably also be taxed under the "subsidy" heading in any case.

6. Where a price is fixed, either on a per unit delivery, or on an overall contractual basis, and it is not possible for the funder unilaterally to reduce the value of the price. In a normal "bargain" whereby a supply would be made, the contract would stipulate the price, rather than stating that "up to £x" will be paid. Thus, one would not expect the payment merely to cover costs incurred, but

rather would expect the full payment to be made whether or not there was a surplus generated by it.

7. One would not expect to see a grant agreement hedged with conditions that it would only be paid if the grantor finds that he has sufficient resources, and may be reduced where resources become unavailable, as one would expect a contract for the delivery of a service to involve a fixed price struck for that particular service.

8. The agreement would not include a raft of terms which tend to arise in grant agreements, concerning such things as equal opportunity employment, ethical sourcing of materials and proposals for extending the life of the project after the funding is no longer available.

9. It is often said that, where the deliverables under an agreement have to be made by the charity, or else it is open to being sued for non-delivery, that indicates a contract. By contrast, if all the funder can do is criticise the charity for failing to perform the activity, and reduce the grant accordingly, then this does not indicate a contract for providing services. Sadly, this rather begs the question itself, namely, can the charity be sued? It would probably require a legal opinion in each case as to whether that was likely, and there must be cases where there would be some degree of uncertainty. Whilst it is a worthwhile test to keep in mind, it is not as useful as it seems at first sight.

10. The provision of incidental benefits to the funder, such as acknowledgment of a commercial nature which is of commercial benefit, will render the payment taxable in any case.

11. If the funder issues a tender document asking charities to bid, and particularly if they need not be charities to bid, then this would strongly suggest that the service is being procured for consideration. Yet, even here, there is a high risk of confusion. It often happens that a funder will put out a "tender" asking charities to bid for pots of grant money for their own solutions to broadly identified problems. This is not the same thing as

issuing a specified service delivery for tender against particular commercial criteria. It is therefore possible to appear to tender for what is in effect grant funding for one's own project as distinct from tendering to win a contract for a particular service delivery.

12. If an organisation such as a government department sets up an agency or quango to carry out a function, and then votes resources to that organisation, it is unlikely, despite the specific nature of the benefit to that government department derived from the arrangement, that there is service provision by the agency. That is because there was no choice on the part of the agency to carry out the activity, since it was set up explicitly to perform that activity. In order for there to be some prospect that there is a supply which is within the scope of business, both parties have to have a choice as to whether to undertake the activity. Where there is compulsion, it seems unlikely that there would be sufficient consensual behaviour to indicate a business activity. That said, of course, there is no reason to assume, just because there is potential consensus, that this is a positive indicator towards there being a business activity, because it is possible to turn down a grant or not to agree to the terms of a grant.

13. A potential "weak indicator" is the language of the agreement. In theory, the way you describe the arrangements does not itself tell you what the arrangements are, and "tags" are unimportant when considering interpretation for VAT purposes. That said, as a "tiebreaker" in certain situations, the language deployed in the agreement may be decisive. Thus, if it is described as a subcontractor agreement, or the outcomes are described as services delivered, or the payment is described as a fee, or consideration, or some similar commercial description, then this nudges the position towards it being a business activity. The converse is true of phraseologies such as "grant",

"milestones", and "outcomes/impacts". However, far too many grant agreements deploy both sets of language indiscriminately, and thus appear to face both ways at the same time.

It is not possible to turn this into a checklist or scoring regime which will give a definitive outcome. All of the above indicators have to be considered as part of a broader picture. There is no choice but to "stand back" and view everything holistically. There is a strong element of subjective impression in determining whether an activity is funded by grant, or is service delivery in return for consideration, and the most important thing is to give it appropriate levels of consideration and thought in order to be able to defend any decision that is taken.

In January 2018, HMRC published long awaited guidance in their manuals (VATSC 51600 – 51900) concerning the above analysis, which is required reading. It broadly follows the above approach.

In line with the theme of this book in general, if in doubt it is a matter to be referred to HMRC Enquiries, particularly where it makes the difference between registering or not registering for VAT.

Reliance on "predominant concern"

Between the High Court decision in *Yarburgh (EWHC 2201)* in 2001 and the Court of Appeal 2016 decision in *Longridge,* many charities relied on the *Lord Fisher* tests to argue that their true purpose was not to make "supplies" for a charge, but merely to seek funding for their charitable work by charging consumers, and were therefore not "in business". It seems that this argument is now unlikely to work. It may continue to apply, however, to small charities with special social aims, although we await HMRC comment on that at the time of writing.

In many cases the classification of such supplies as "business" simply means that they become exempt and does not affect the registration status of the charity, but this is not always the case.

Cases: *Yarburgh Children's Trust v C&E Commrs* [2002] EWHC 2201; *Longridge on the Thames* [2016] EWCA Civ 930

5.3 Illegal activity

For obvious reasons this is not a subject that needs to be dwelt upon. However, the basic position is that activity which is illegal by reference to circumstance (e.g. selling a service for which the seller has failed to be properly regulated) may still fall within the scope of VAT. But selling a service which is illegal from all angles (e.g. assassinating someone in return for payment) would not be regarded as falling within the scope of VAT.

6. Agent or principal?

6.1 Introduction

The distinction between acting as agent or principal, in relation to the question of whether or when a business must register for VAT, cannot be over-emphasised. This is because VAT registration thresholds are measured in the value of the supply made, i.e. turnover, and not any profit that is derived from the supply. It is therefore fairly obvious that a person who buys someone else's goods or services must make a supply to the value both of the purchase price and profit added, whereas a person who acts as an agent/intermediary, and charges a commission to either the buyer or seller or perhaps both, will only make a supply to the value of the profit.

Example

Gomez Ltd purchases cleaning services from Egerton Ltd, and sells them to a variety of its customers. Gomez Ltd enters into contracts where it is clear that it is procuring Egerton Ltd's services, and providing the combined cleaning service to all of its various customers. Its own profit margin may give rise to an income of, say, £50,000 per year. However, it may be turning over in excess of £300,000 per year, since it is selling Egerton Ltd's services as part of its service.

Contrast this with the situation where Gomez Ltd can regard itself as no more than an agent for the parties. In this case, Egerton Ltd makes separate supplies to all of Gomez Ltd's "customers". Gomez Ltd charges either Egerton Ltd, or each customer, a commission for his services in making the arrangements. The aggregate of those commissions is £50,000. Gomez Ltd has no obligation to register for VAT under the current thresholds.

There may be no other difference between the two kinds of business model than the legal arrangements between the parties (although those must have substantive legal impact), and thus a business which is essentially the same would be VAT registered in one instance and non-VAT registered in the other.

6.2 Case law

6.2.1 *Overview*

There have been numerous cases determining the difference between an agent and a principal in such situations, and perhaps the most well-known are the following three:

- Spearmint Rhino;
- Secret Hotels 2 (aka Med Hotels); and
- A1 Lofts.

Cases: *A1 Lofts* [2010] UKFTT 581 (TC); *Secret Hotels 2* [2014] UKSC 16; *Spearmint Rhino Ventures (UK) Ltd v R&C Commrs* [2007] EWHC 613, [2007] STC 1252

6.2.2 *Spearmint Rhino*

This sticks in the mind because it was a case concerning "gentlemen's entertainment services".

Spearmint Rhino is a club where women entertain men in small booths where various dances are performed to the patrons. The patron has to pay an entrance fee to the establishment, and this was regarded by the Spearmint Rhino venue as its own turnover. A further amount was paid by patrons to each dancer, from which the dancer paid part to Spearmint Rhino and retained the balance.

The question was whether, in reality, Spearmint Rhino was charging the patrons for the dance activity as well as for admission to the premises (in which case the entire turnover generated by the venue would be regarded as the value of taxable supplies), or whether, conversely, the dance element was provided directly by each dancer to the patrons, and that the amount taken by Spearmint Rhino was a facilities charge made to each self employed dancer (which would be the only taxable turnover from the fees collected by the dancer).

It is worth noting that, first, we are not concerned whether the dancers are self employed as such. All that counts is whether they are selling their services to the club proprietor, for onward sale, as part of a bundled package to the patrons, or whether the club proprietor is selling a service to the self employed dancer. It is also of limited relevance that the patron paid the money to the dancer as opposed to paying it to Spearmint Rhino in a manner which did not involve the dancer handling the cash. On the detailed facts overall, and perhaps by a close margin, this case came down in favour of the dancers making direct supplies to their clients.

It illustrates an important consideration in this, which is that if the workers maintain a certain level of autonomy as to how much work they do, the circumstances in which they are prepared to work, and precisely what activities they are prepared to engage in, then this would indicate that they have some degree of separation from the party that would call itself an "agent". If, on the other hand, the service provided allows relatively little differentiation between service providers, and they must do effectively as the intermediary directs, then this is more likely to indicate that the supply is one made by a principal to the final consumer, and thus increases the turnover accordingly. (Where the extent of this is indicative of the service provider being actually employed by the "intermediary", which is a wholly different area but based on similar considerations, then that would certainly point to the whole supply being made by the ostensible intermediary. At the time of writing, a case is in progress that seeks to establish whether Uber, whose drivers have been held by the EAT to be "employees", should follow this principle.)

The details in the contract are potentially indicative of one or other state of affairs, but a written contractual term does not define it beyond all doubt. As a general rule, written contractual terms should be accepted as the likely best guide to interpretation, but if they are clearly overridden by real circumstances, or they are open to varying interpretations, then they will have a more limited impact on the overall interpretation.

Case: *Spearmint Rhino Ventures (UK) Ltd v R&C Commrs* [2007] EWHC 613, [2007] STC 1252

6.2.3 Secret Hotels 2

This case involved four decisions, two for HMRC and two for the taxpayer, ending in a Supreme Court decision in early 2014 in the taxpayer's favour.

The issue here is whether the Appellant, Secret Hotels 2, which procures accommodation overseas for its patrons, acts as a principal in procuring that accommodation and selling a package to the traveller, or acts as an agent on behalf of the hotel and intermediates between it and the traveller. In this case, it was not about whether of Secret Hotels 2 was VAT registered (as it was anyway), but rather about the liability of the supply. However, it is relevant to this particular subject, in regard to the principles that are set out.

The big question was whether the terms of the contract were determinative, or whether other aspects had to be brought into consideration. It is not disputed that where the activities depart from the contractual terms in an explicit kind of way, it is the actual activities that determine the nature of the supply, rather than the contract. In the case of *Secret Hotels 2*, it was possible to interpret the activities as departing from the contractual terms when viewed holistically, but, when atomised and compared to the contractual terms, there was a great deal more similarity. In other words, the sum of the activities' parts may point in one direction (though that would be a subjective view), but each individual component may not itself appear to displace the contractual arrangements.

That was important in this case because the contract explicitly stated that Secret Hotels 2 acted as an agent on behalf of each hotel. The first-tier tribunal and the Court of Appeal decided to stand back from the situation and view the entire activity as a whole. They pointed out a variety of aspects which did not appear to be indicative of Secret Hotels 2 merely acting as an intermediary. It appeared to be more heavily involved than that, and particularly took on liabilities that were more indicative of it acting as a principal (it tended to bear risk). The upper tribunal (with the intervening decision) took the view that the contract was not contradicted by the activities if each and every activity carried out was consistent with the contract, even if one might have determined the position rather differently if viewing it as a whole.

The Supreme Court sought to reconcile these approaches, and leant more towards the view that the terms of the contract should settle the status as long as they reflected "economic reality" and were not decisively undermined by the operational conduct of the business. The taxpayer's assertion that it was an agent was accepted.

Case: *Secret Hotels 2* [2014] UKSC 16

6.2.4 A1 Lofts

This is a case where a party which could be broadly described as a "project manager" made arrangements to convert people's lofts into extra accommodation within their houses.

A1 Lofts procured all of the various workmen who were to carry out the activity, ensured a workable plan, priced up the job, and then offered its customers the entire package for a given fee. A1 Lofts was not registered for VAT, and did not make enough income, if one considers its share of the turnover separately, to require it to register. But, if one treated it as a principal, such that it sold the supplies of the various workmen in one package to each customer, then it was over the VAT registration threshold.

The tribunal (following its reconsideration after the upper tribunal remitted it for further hearing) drew the firm conclusion that A1 Lofts was not acting as an agent but rather as a principal. It was felt that a complete obligation was entered into between A1 Lofts and the customer, and that A1 Lofts would have to put right anything which the workmen had done wrong, to provide a complete loft conversion service. It was not acting, according to the tribunal, in a fiduciary capacity on behalf of either the purchaser or the supplier, but was managing the job sufficiently intensively to give rise to something more involved than merely making arrangements and acting for one party or the other. It could, of course, be argued that a good agent takes such a role in any case, since to appear to be such arm's length removed from either the seller or the buyer, would be commercially impossible.

Case: *A1 Lofts* [2010] UKFTT 581 (TC)

6.2.5 Making a decision in practice

Whilst these, and several other cases, do not provide a particularly clear picture, and the distinction between an agent and a principal is still a very debatable point, perhaps the following practical considerations can help to determine the matter as closely as is usually necessary:

- An agent's primary role is to connect one party with another, and then to stand back and let the two get on with it. Any "agent" which becomes continuously involved in the arrangements could instead be regarded as a principal in the supply chain.

- Risk is a major factor. Although an agent faces risk in due course from reputational damage if the supplier that he appoints fails to perform (or the customer fails to pay), he is not immediately at risk for failure to produce the service or goods (or for them to be paid for), since he has merely introduced the parties to one another. In general, HMRC will not accept that a person is an agent if he has shouldered anything more than a nominal commercial risk. In particular, if he has to "indemnify" the supplier for non-payment for the services, this suggests that the "agent" is really buying that service himself.

- An agent who goes too far in promising to the customer that he will step in to rectify any fault on the part of the supplier, or shift the contract from one supplier to another at the behest of the customer, runs significant risk of being seen to be a principal. An agent would not normally intervene in such a way (though that in itself is a fiercely debated point).

- An agent who has powers of not remitting the payment in question back to the principal for whom he appears to act, on the basis of the work not being done to the right standard, for instance, is rarely going to be regarded as an agent of the supplier, since he should act entirely on behalf of his client (whichever party that may be), and not take the view that he can direct his client to do various things at his own behest. But it could be consistent with him being an agent of the customer, so the detail of the relationship needs to be taken into account.

- The payment terms can be indicative of one or the other state. Whilst it is possible for an agent to handle money on behalf of his principal, and remit a balance, net of his own commission, any suggestion that he has a power to withhold payment entirely, or either reduce or increase it according to his own view of the position, does not indicate an agent's activities. He is more likely to be regarded as a principal in such situations. Even the timing of passing

85

over customer payments could have an impact on the interpretation.

- Where the agent is absolutely integral to bringing everything together in such a way that, without him, everything would fail as a matter of course, then an agent is at greater risk of being regarded as a principal. Thus, although an agent can "pull strings" to orchestrate several suppliers making a supply to one party, the suppliers nonetheless have to come together without him being personally involved in anything other than an intermediary type of capacity. It follows, therefore, that it is hard for a builder to regard himself as an agent when procuring the services of other workmen if those other workmen effectively have to work through the builder in order for there to be a product to sell to the customer.

How accountants set out the accounts can be vital to getting this right. An accountant cannot turn a person into an agent simply by only recording his "commission" as turnover. However, if he wrongly records the "commission" as the only turnover, he can wrongly mislead his client into thinking that he was not registerable. In that case, the self assessment tax return would not show the whole story and the client would be open to significant risk of a belated VAT registration scenario. This might have been avoided if the accountant had been sufficiently inquisitive as to all of the arrangements which may have indicated that the business was acting as a principal rather than an agent.

As a general point, it is less risky to assume that one is a principal unless there are very clear indications that one is an agent. Agents who do not fit neatly into trades which are habitually carried on by agents (for example, estate agents and certain kinds of high street travel agent) are at greater risk of being found to be wrong, thus leading to a VAT registration difficulty.

6.3   Agent acting as principal

This is also called "blind agency" or "undisclosed agency". It relates to cases where the agent does not reveal to the customer that he is an agent of the supplier. He pretends (so to speak) to be the principal and thus the supplier to the customer. This is usually to keep the supplier's identity secret, but it can arise in cases where the customer knows who the supplier is, but it is convenient to represent the situation as the agent being a participant in the actual supply chain rather than merely a facilitator.

Where such an agent handles the sale of goods, then he is deemed automatically to act as a principal for VAT purposes. Where he handles the supply of services HMRC can choose to treat the supply as though he were the principal for VAT purposes.

This means that an entity can appear to meet all the criteria of being an agent, but if it specifically "holds out" that it is selling the goods or services, it is deemed to generate the full turnover, at least in the case of goods, and potentially where services are concerned.

Law: VATA 1994, s. 47

6.4 Tour operators

An exception to the above debate arises under the Tour Operators Margin Scheme ("TOMS"). TOMS in fact affects every entity that makes supplies within its definition, not merely recognised tour operators. Defining a TOMS situation is a subject in itself, but for present purposes it is sufficient to describe it as a case where the supplier purchases travel supplies which he sells on as a principal in an unaltered state (e.g. hotel rooms). Under TOMS he is deemed to treat only his margin as the taxable supply, and not the entire turnover. This is also true for VAT registration and thus contradicts the basic principle referred to above.

Law: VATA 1994, s. 53; SI 1987/1806

7. Profit or consideration?

7.1 Joint business activity

A common business model is for parties to come together in a joint venture, sharing the costs, and, they hope, sharing the profit in pre-ordained ratios. It is also common to believe that the amounts shared are merely a profit distribution and therefore outside the scope of VAT. This is based on the view that neither party makes a supply to the other, because they are both in a joint endeavour, and they are both seeking simply to make supplies to other third parties.

Leaving aside, for the moment, whether, jointly, they are making taxable supplies, the question remains as to whether this analysis of the share of proceeds being "profit" has any impact on the VAT position.

Whilst profit distribution is indeed outside the scope of VAT, on the basis that it is not consideration for a supply, one has to be sure that one is dealing with pure profit distribution. Indeed, a better way to think of this is not to ask "am I making a profit?" but rather "is this money I am receiving in return for something I am doing for the other party?". This is because profit is only regarded as not being consideration when that is precisely the case; that is, there is nothing being supplied in return for the profit. Profit, therefore, can only be a return on capital invested in a business. It can arise as profits earned through a genuine partnership. It can arise as dividends paid to shareholders. Anything else is unlikely to be regarded as outside the scope, unless it can be shown not to be in consideration of some supply to another party.

So, where would there be a situation where two parties coming together, in order to make the best of a mutual business opportunity, might be regarded as making supplies to each other?

Example

A "bricks and mortar" retailer decides that he wants to set up an internet operation. This requires a significant amount of investment which he believes is too risky to carry out on his own. He contacts an internet platform entrepreneur who agrees to assist in setting this up. The retailer contributes the underpinning of the business, being the fact that he has stock, the brand, and the general "goodwill" of the business. The internet platform provider provides precisely that, an internet platform, along with the know-how to make it more likely to be viable. They agree a cost price of the stock, and various other costs as being costs of the business to be subtracted from the turnover in order to devise a "profit". With good luck, they do generate such a profit, and their agreement is, say, to split this 50:50. Do both of them simply make a profit (outside the scope of VAT), or is there any consideration for a service?

Plainly, one or other of the parties has to be selling the relevant goods to the final consumer, which will be within the scope of VAT as though they were being sold in the shop. That would usually be the retailer himself. If that is the case, then they are not operating as a partnership (though they could have set it up as one, of course), since only the retailer is making the sales of the products. By definition this must mean that the internet platform provider is providing a service to the retailer. The reference to "profit" is merely a mechanism for remunerating him for his services. In effect he is on a success based contract, which is keyed directly into the financial success of the operation. His "profit share" is consideration for taxable services, and thus adds towards the registration threshold.

7.2   Land

A more traditional scenario involves developing land.

Example

A land owner (which is defined for VAT purposes as the beneficial owner) has land to sell, but lacks the expertise to develop plans for selling it. Alternatively, a land owner wishes to sell it, but cannot find a developer who is prepared simply to buy the land and then take all of the risk. In either scenario, the land owner and the promoter/developer come together in order to make the most of the business opportunity. As in the previous example, they agree which costs are regarded as costs of their joint operation, and that will help determine any profit arising from the sale of the land, or the sale of the units that are developed upon the land (or in more sophisticated cases, perhaps some kind of "earn out" based upon rental yields).

It is tempting for the promoter/developer to take the view that he is achieving mere profit share, and thus his income is outside the scope of VAT. That will almost never be the case. A promoter, for instance, usually has no rights in the land (though that is not always so), but rather acts as a form of highly expert property consultant and negotiator. His service is therefore taxable, and the value of the consideration he receives is dependant upon a notional "profit". Where a builder acts in this role, he will usually be regarded, within the terms of the contract, as providing construction services to the land owner, since the land owner finally sells the developed properties (or enters into rental leases for them). The builder is thus providing some kind of taxable service (though it may be zero-rated as new residential construction, but this in itself could give rise to a need to register for VAT).

On the other hand, the arrangement could be configured such that the owner sells the land to the developer, who sells the completed properties, and then pays the land owner an amount by reference to his "profit". In that situation the land owner will have made a supply which is probably exempt from VAT (being land), but could be taxable (if opted into VAT by the land owner). He will not be merely receiving a profit share, because the payment has been made in consideration of an asset transfer from him to the developer. The developer then sells the completed properties to the public.

One exception to this was the somewhat unusual case of *Latchmere*. This may not prove to be a precedent that others follow. Latchmere was a developer who entered into a similar arrangement with the land owner, but he had both the right to purchase the land, and the obligation to purchase the land if no other purchaser could be found. Thus he had a significant right over the land himself by means of the contract. In the end, the land owner sold the land to a third party and remitted the balance to Latchmere. Latchmere's claim was not that it had received profit share, but rather that it had made an exempt supply. In the circumstances, the tribunal agreed that the supply was an exempt right over land which it had jointly provided with the land owner to the final consumer. Thus, whilst the supply was not made to the land owner in this case, even so, the payment was regarded as consideration rather than as "profit share".

The main tribunal cases which have underpinned this interpretation are: *Strathearn Gordon Associates Ltd, Keydon Estates Ltd, Fivegrange Ltd*, and the above mentioned *Latchmere Properties Ltd*.

Of course, matters are very different if the parties set up a separate limited company of which both are shareholders, or go into a formal partnership arrangement, whereby they contribute their resources and assets into a joint structure where they share both profits and the potential for losses on a joint and several basis. In that case, however, that particular entity will be making the supply to the final consumer.

Finally, joint title holders to the land, whilst not being technically a partnership, tend to be treated by HMRC as a partnership, and therefore their proceeds would normally be regarded as outside the scope of VAT, but they would then register for VAT (if applicable) as a partnership in order to account for VAT on any sale they make.[1]

Cases: *Strathearn Gordon Associates Ltd* (VTD 1884); *Keydon Estates Ltd* (VTD 4471); *Fivegrange Ltd* (VTD 5338); *Latchmere Properties Ltd* EWHC 133, Ch D [2005] STC 731

---

[1] The difficulties created by joint ownership of a business are covered in the next chapter, on business fragmentation.

8. Business fragmentation

8.1 HMRC defences

The title of this section may appear pejorative and judgemental. However, it is the most common way of describing a situation which HMRC perceive to be an abuse. Another phrase that is deployed is "business splitting".

The idea, here, is that steps may be taken to split a single business between two entities or more in order that one or more of them should avoid having to be VAT registered. As mentioned elsewhere, the general rule is that it is the legal entity which is registered for VAT (irrespective of how many businesses it contains), and not the business as such. Thus, unless there are safeguards, it is unduly tempting to try to split a business down the middle in order to avoid VAT registration, by partitioning it between various different legal entities.

HMRC have two defences against this:

- To issue a "direction" under which they can deem more than one entity to be operating as though it were one entity and to have to register accordingly.
- To argue that, in substance and reality, the entities are a kind of partnership which should be treated as though it were one legal entity and is registerable accordingly.

These two principles are separate, but closely aligned. It is important to be able to distinguish between the two, since various points of detail are different as between them.

8.2 Directions to be treated as one entity

8.2.1 Introduction

HMRC can issue a direction upon more than one entity to be treated as though it is one for VAT registration purposes alone, but only in circumstances where it perceives there to be an artificial fragmentation of a single business. The direction can only have prospective effect, so that it does not catch situations where the fragmentation has occurred over prior years, and accordingly does not give rise to belated VAT registration. Because of this, it is not the most powerful tool imaginable, and we will come on to an approach HMRC have been known to take in order to try to circumvent this weakness.

The direction will only be issued where one or more of the entities is not registered, and where they are regarded by HMRC as being closely connected by financial, economic and organisational links.

It is worth looking at these in a little more detail.

Law: VATA 1994, Sch. 1, para. 2

8.2.2   The tests

Financial links

These are links between the two or more entities which relate to flows of money, and literal financial support. Do they support each other by sharing a single resource of capital and cash? Does one entity need the specific financial support of another (although that is similar to the first)? Does a single shareholder or group of shareholders benefit from all of the proceeds of the entities, such that it scarcely matters whether one makes a loss and the other a profit because the outcome for the owners is the same?

Economic links

HMRC look to see if the same "economic objectives" are being sought by all of the entities (though it is difficult to see what is meant by this because profit is likely to be the economic objective of almost any entity). They look to see if the activities of the businesses benefit each other (though that would also be true of unrelated separate businesses, such as a parade of unrelated shops, or co-located symbiotic businesses, such as a logistics business being located next to a distribution business). And finally whether they are supplying goods or services to the same customers (although, again, for obvious reasons, unrelated businesses could be doing precisely that, such as shops within shops, market stall holders, catering establishments in sports centres etc.).

Organisational links

HMRC look at whether the entities are sharing resources, often including premises, staff, equipment, and an overarching management structure. This, it seems, is getting rather closer to the nub of the issue. It is difficult to fragment a business into separate entities without compromising efficiency if you are having to equip all of the entities with their own set of resources and are thus duplicating effort.

In looking at these tests, HMRC have commented about particular businesses in the following way.

Franchises

A genuine commercial franchise operation is acceptable, but one that has been set up merely in order to avoid VAT would not be. This is a strange point of view, since most franchise operations are set up with the view that different owners will operate the franchisee outlets in order to provide capital for the franchise business, and therefore they are unconnected in ownership terms. Anything other than that would not be a normal franchise model.

Hairdressers

HMRC are concerned to ensure that individual hair stylists do not seek to set themselves up as ostensibly separate businesses unless they are genuinely providing their services directly to customers without undue support from the infrastructure of the business. This is a curious preoccupation when related to the issue of fragmenting businesses. The point should be dealt with on the basis of who is supplying what to whom, which is governed by other principles (and, in particular, see the discussion of the issue in regard to the case of *Spearmint Rhino* at **6.2.2**). Nonetheless, HMRC see this as a fragmentation issue, and are unwilling to see separate businesses arising from otherwise unconnected hair stylists where they:

- are not responsible for keeping their own records;
- are not responsible for their own health and safety procedures;
- do not have separate insurance policies;

- have some protection from the salon itself from any losses that might be made;
- have no control over the prices they set;
- are subject to an anti-competition ethos within the salon;
- are not allowed to appoint a locum; and
- do not hold themselves out as being separate for the purposes of legal service of notices, etc.

HMRC go on to say that each individual's part of the salon should be separately accessible and that the stylist should be able to access his part of the premises at any time, irrespective of the normal opening hours. The stylist ought to have his own particular clients (which for hair stylists tends to be the case irrespective of the business model) and his own collecting box for cash.

The above is expressed somewhat briefly, and there is more material available from HMRC on this. However, it is clear from HMRC's comments that they are seeking to apply a "substance and reality" test to determine whether there is one business owned by the salon, or several owned by individual operators.

Taxis

Self employed taxi drivers will not be seen as forming part of a wider business unless the circumstances otherwise seem to suggest this.

HMRC

When looking at HMRC's guidance, it is surprising perhaps that it is not more forensic in regard to the kind of arrangements that are seen as abusive. One would have thought that the key indications of artificially separated businesses would be as follows:

- a high degree of mutual ownership between the entities, perhaps at an apex, pointing to the possibility that one business mind controls all of the entities;
- interactions between the separate entities, whether on an organisational or financial basis, that would be unsustainable and unrealistic as between true commercial third parties;

- an inability by the customer to discern that he is dealing with more than one entity, or if he does, that it would be obvious that it was somewhat contrived;
- the sale of services or goods where a customer would plainly not receive the full product if he were only to buy from one or other of the entities, such that that would be an unrealistic selling proposition;
- "holding out" to both suppliers and customers, and potentially to investors, as being one activity rather than several.

On the other hand, it is important to consider whether HMRC may try to launch an argument that the entities are engaged in a single holistic business when they are not.

Example

Five separate companies own five separate launderettes in five different locations, all under common ownership, and sharing the same brand name. This will tempt HMRC to regard the arrangement as artificial business splitting. That could be true if the launderettes shared the same staff (though they are likely to be separately staffed for geographic reasons). It could also be true if they shared the same bank account (but that would be easy to change, and is inherently somewhat unlikely).

If all of their administration was done jointly this is a weak indicator of fragmentation, since there is no particular reason why they could not consume management supplies from a holding company as is commonly the case in a group of companies. Plainly, each is separately operable and its customers will perceive each launderette as a separate establishment. It would be abusive of HMRC to try to argue that these businesses are indivisible and constitute a single business.

By contrast, where the same person ultimately owns a single catering establishment, where one entity does the wet supplies and the other does the dry supplies, or where one entity provides all of the catering and the other lets the premises for events, one can see that HMRC would be on stronger ground to allege that there is a single indivisible business going on.

8.2.3 Impact of direction

The direction is communicated in a letter sent individually to each participant, but naming all of the other participants. This letter sets a date with effect from which all of them will be registered jointly. That date can be no earlier than the date of the direction. HMRC will then cancel any VAT registration separately carried on in the name of any one of the parties, so that the joint registration can supersede this registration. The direction advises all of the entities that they will be jointly and severally liable for the tax due from the VAT registration from the relevant date onwards.

A curious aspect of this situation can arise where one or more of the legal entities in question is registered for VAT, though the others are not. It may be registered because it carries on a variety of businesses, only one of which relates to this potential fragmentation scenario. Since all of the entities will be treated as forming the same VAT registration, the other unrelated businesses carried out by an entity caught by a direction notice would be subsumed within the joint VAT registration, and all of the entities are jointly and severally liable for all of the activities of each other, even if some activities are unrelated to the amalgamated business. This may require the need to review whether to hive off such entirely separate activities into a separate company, such that the VAT registration covering the businesses which are accused of artificial fragmentation is entirely separate.

8.3 Retrospective application

As mentioned, the weakness of the direction is that it can only deal with collecting the relevant tax going forward. However, HMRC have occasionally tried to argue that a business is in any case indivisible and does not require a direction in order to be registered as a single entity. This can only be based on some kind of assumption that the different persons or entities that were undertaking the business were acting in partnership, although they will not have had a partnership deed.

The benefit of this argument is that it can give rise to retrospective VAT registration where, taken together, the business activities exceeded the turnover threshold. Yet it appears to fly in the face of the general legal position, which is that only the entity can be registered, and not the business (the HMRC direction being a deeming provision that overrides that specific rule). For this reason, HMRC would probably be reluctant to launch such an argument except in cases where the degree of inter-relationship is so profound that it appears completely contrived to regard it as a separate operation. In particular, where there is joint procurement, joint financing, and a single set of books which may be artificially split at some point to give the similitude of separation, this will look like a single business operation which has been split in a crude and artificial manner and therefore could be regarded as a single entity from inception (in essence, a kind of "partnership"). This is reinforced if customers can perceive no difference between one activity and another, and are induced to think they are dealing with one proprietor.[1]

By contrast, even where there are close relationships between the subject matter of the businesses, and potentially close social relationships (such as married couples), if there is separate accounting, separate bookkeeping, separate banking and procurement arrangements, and if the products have some degree of separation in nature, it will be difficult for HMRC to sustain the view that they are a single business even if they have significant inter-relations such as could make them subject to a direction notice.

That said, the *Belcher* case, decided in 2017, suggested that even where some clear indicators of partnership arise, HMRC may face challenges. Mr and Mrs Belcher both operated hair care services from the same building, one being a gentlemen's barbers, and the other a ladies' hairdressers. The single building had separate operational parts which were respectively used by the two individuals. They operated one bank account between them. Their retained external accountant took the initiative of drawing up partnership accounts for them.

But when HMRC alleged that the two had failed to register for VAT in circumstances where they were both, individually, below the thresholds, the Tribunal accepted the spouses' argument that they

---

[1] It should be noted that the mere absence of a partnership deed (or agreement) does not in law mean that a partnership does not exist, so this, on its own, would not be a sufficient defence.

were individual proprietors with independent businesses. Apart from being married, both trading in the hair sector, and sharing a bank account for convenience' sake, nothing linked the businesses. The partnership accounts were held to be an error by an accountant who had jumped to conclusions, and had not been reined in by his lay clients.

They could perhaps count themselves lucky, but it makes a salutary case for both sides.

Another example is the case of *Mr and Mrs Townsend*, albeit now nearly 20 years old.

Both were interested in pottery. Mr Townsend (who was not registered) made high value crafted pots that could sell for many tens of pounds. Mrs Townsend bought merchandise to sell, and did a certain amount of superficial decoration of mass market ceramics, all of which was aimed at a much cheaper market. Mrs Townsend operated a shop which sold her products in a particular tourist area. Mr Townsend sold his products partly through the shop, but partly by reputation and direct sale. Mrs Townsend charged Mr Townsend a commission for the sales she carried out on his behalf, but they kept their other business affairs separate. HMRC sought to argue that this husband and wife business was one pottery retail business which could not be treated as separate. The tribunal decided that this was wrong and that the businesses were sufficiently separate and not automatically to be regarded as operating through a single entity. In other words, they did not see the husband and wife as a "husband and wife partnership".

Cases: *Dennis Townsend and Maureen Townsend* (VTD 17081); *Belcher v HMRC* [2017] UKFTT 427 (TC)

8.4 General observations

As you might imagine, in a case concerning fragmentation, there is no prescribed formula for determining how successful HMRC would be in challenging the position, and the devil is always in the detail. That said, there is a great deal of public pressure on HMRC to ensure that *bona fide* businesses being run on a conventional basis and thus falling within the scope of VAT, do not suffer commercial disadvantage by having to compete with fragmented businesses which appear not to have to pay VAT simply because they are split artificially between different legal entities. It is, arguably, the high VAT registration threshold that gives rise to this difficulty. So, one can expect HMRC to be vigilant particularly if they receive complaints from neighbouring traders.

In the spirit of the general theme of this book, it would be best if any contrived arrangements were abandoned and the business became registered for VAT, rather than trying to be "clever" and seek an unfair advantage over more conventionally operated businesses. That said, there will be cases where HMRC see an abuse that is not there.

9. Voluntary registration

9.1 Reasons to register voluntarily

It seems counter-intuitive to register voluntarily for VAT before one actually has to do so, but in fact it is very common for various reasons. These are:

1. to enjoy the fiscal and commercial advantages identified in the opening chapters of this book;
2. to ensure that VAT recoverable on start-up costs can be reclaimed in situations where it is inevitable that the business will exceed the thresholds in due course;
3. to avoid waiting too long and failing to register on time.

It is not possible to register voluntarily for VAT if there is no intention to make taxable supplies. However, an intention to make taxable supplies could include an intention to make deemed supplies, such as to import services which are subject to the reverse charge. It is not immediately obvious why that would be to any advantage, however, since there would then be no actual taxable supplies against which to set VAT the business incurs on the deemed liability.

An activity has to amount to a business in order to be taxable, so voluntary registration would not be open where an entity makes supplies which would be taxable if it were a business, but where it does not in fact amount to a business (in respect of which please refer to **Chapter 5** concerning the definition of a "business"). In particular, HMRC are often unwilling to register "hobby businesses" where the taxable supplies are exceeded by the VAT-bearing costs incurred, thus giving a fiscal advantage to the hobbyist.

HMRC have a particular track record of not agreeing to register entities which purchase such things as light aircraft and yacht/canal boats with a view to arranging for a certain amount of income to be generated, on the side, through taxable lettings. HMRC's concern, in that case, is that the VAT incurred on the vehicle is substantial, whereas the value of taxable supplies that would be made is relatively low. This, in their view, points towards the making of a private purchase rather than buying a business asset.

HMRC would tend to challenge situations where there is just one vehicle (see *Three H Aircraft Hire*), or where the owner merely hands the vehicle over to a commercial charter company in order for that company to seek customers for charter of the vehicle. HMRC view this as too passive an activity to amount to a business. It would require the owner of the vehicle to make day-to-day (or at least higher level) strategic decisions, as to the customers to accept for the charter in order for it to amount to a business. This view is strange since the *Principal VAT Directive* makes clear that receiving income from the exploitation of assets falls within the scope of an "economic activity".

Law: VATA 1994, Sch. 1, para. 9; EC/2006/112
Case: *Three H Aircraft Hire v C&E Commrs* [1982] STC 653

9.2 Land and property

It is sometimes the case that land which is held privately is earmarked for sale for commercial use, perhaps to a property developer. Sale of development land is exempt from VAT unless the owner exercises an option to tax under VATA 1994, Sch. 10. Thus the legislation gives an effective choice to the seller as to whether to treat himself as falling within the scope of taxable supplies, by making a specific option to tax, or to leave his land un-opted so that only exempt supplies are made. As to which choice he will adopt, this would depend on the extent of the VAT-bearing costs incurred. If he is going to employ an estate agent or land promoter to act on his behalf, the VAT on the costs could be considerable, and if the developer to whom he is selling the land can reclaim the VAT then (SDLT considerations aside) it may well be preferable to opt to tax voluntarily and register for VAT.

A potential question arises as to whether, even having been opted into tax, the sale of the land is carried on in the course or furtherance of a business. HMRC used to take the view that the sale of a single property was not in itself a business. Of course, for the most part, any private sales tend to be exempt, and a probable policy reason for the exempting of sales of land and real estate is in order to avoid any borderline situations between taxable business sales and outside scope non-business sales.

Some 20 years or so ago, HMRC began to accept that the sale of a single property was a business activity, and that options to tax applied to single properties would be regarded as bringing the sale within the scope of VAT. When one considers that the entire purpose of the option to tax is to avoid a VAT burden on the cost of property until it is supplied to the final consumer, and that the sale of land under an option to tax would only logically be made when it is to be sold to a commercial user (so the land forms part of a business supply chain), one can see that this is the application of good common sense. The writer is not aware of any situation where an owner who sold land having opted to tax, and applied for VAT registration on that basis, was refused registration and denied input tax recovery simply on the basis that the land had not been exploited for business use beforehand, or that its sale did not amount to a business proposition.

9.3 Proving intention to trade

HMRC will be reluctant to allow voluntary registration based on the mere intention to trade where there is no objective proof of that. To give them the reassurance they need, a business will need to have drawn up some kind of business plan (or at least financial projections), preferably entered into agreements with suppliers which show that the business will incur costs, and also, where possible, entered into any agreements with potential customers to show that supplies will be made. On the whole, HMRC accept evidence of costs already incurred on tax invoices as determining that a business is genuinely intended.

It is important to apply with an effective date no later than six months after the tax point for services received, or four years after the tax point for goods received. This should be sufficient to preserve the right to recover the VAT. This does not apply to any cost falling within the capital goods scheme, since this cannot be reclaimed if dated before the effective registration date at all. You then need to ensure the effective date is earlier than these costs. That said, the interpretation of these rules is extremely difficult, since the law may well be referring to completed capital items (which have thus been brought into use prior to the date of registration) or, on a stretched interpretation, could include component costs of such a capital item even before it has come into use. The second interpretation defies all logic but is conceivably what is intended.

9.4 Speculative ventures

Certain ventures are entered into in the hope that there is a business opportunity, but this does not always transpire. Sometimes considerable VAT-bearing costs are incurred in pursuit of the objective, but in the end no supplies are made. However, the *Principal VAT Directive* is clear that the activity is deemed to be a business irrespective of the outcome. If its supplies, had it been a successful business, would have been taxable, HMRC cannot deny VAT registration, and the input tax reclaimed need not be reimbursed. This is based on the precedent of *INZO* and *Ghent Coal*, both of which involved abortive plans entered into over several years, with significant costs, but which were upheld as giving rise to a right to register for VAT voluntarily, and reclaim the VAT. (However, if the original intention is replaced by an intention to make exempt supplies, then the input tax is clawed back by HMRC).

Obviously, it helps to register prior to the project becoming abortive, since, if an application to register retrospectively arises after the project is doomed, HMRC will be sceptical whether there was ever any strong intention to carry through with the project. It is therefore important for businesses not to miss their opportunity to register for VAT. Many businesses may wrongly assume that they have to be able to demonstrate being on the cusp of making taxable supplies before they have the right to register. This is a misconception, and they should register as soon as possible in order to secure the best chance of VAT recovery.

Law: EC/2006/112

Cases: *Intercommunale voor Zeewaterontzilting (INZO) v Belgian State* C-110/94, [1996] STC 569; *Belgium v Ghent Coal Terminal NV* C-37/95 [1998] STC 260

9.5 Nature of taxable supplies for purposes of voluntary registration

As mentioned above, a business must make "taxable supplies" in order to be able voluntarily to register for VAT. But in this case, unlike with compulsory VAT registration, "taxable supplies" includes those that would be taxable had they been supplies made in the UK. In other words, an activity which would give rise to taxable supplies made outside the UK, where the income is therefore outside the scope of UK VAT, nonetheless gives rise to a right to register voluntarily for VAT. For this reason it is possible for overseas businesses that make no supplies in the UK to set up physical branches in the UK, register for VAT, and reclaim VAT without any intention of making supplies that would be taxable in the UK.

This principle also extends to so called "specified supplies" which are certain financial services exported to persons outside the EU, which would be exempt if supplied in the UK but are deemed "taxable" (though outside the scope) for the purposes of voluntary registration and input tax recovery.

9.6 Voluntary registration for acquisitions from other EU states

Whilst the general rule is that taxable supplies have to be made to be able voluntarily to register for UK VAT there is in fact another way, though a rare one, in which an entity can qualify, and that is to make acquisitions of goods from the EU. The entity may then choose to register under the acquisitions rules even though not required compulsorily to do so. This is only of any real significance if the rate at which VAT is payable in the UK is lower than that at which it would be payable in the state or states from which the goods are supplied. Thus, a wholly exempt entity that acquires goods at below the compulsory level can in any case register voluntarily to reap the benefit of the lower domestic rate. To stop him "shopping around" for rates, there is a time limit for subsequent de-registration, and this is dealt with in **Chapter 13**. However, once registered under this provision, any UK taxable supplies made by the entity fall subject to a VAT liability.

Law: VATA 1994, Sch. 33, para. 4

9.7 Voluntary registration for distance selling

This is relevant to the debate concerning voluntary registration because it is a matter of choice as to whether to await breaching the various thresholds for compulsory registration or to volunteer from

105

any other point in time to declare tax on one's distance sales in the target country. Thus, if a distance seller from Sweden generates £40,000 of sales to UK consumers he may well wish to register for UK VAT so as to pay at the (currently) lower UK rates of VAT while perhaps keeping the prices the same, thus reducing fiscal cost albeit at an administrative expense. This is the full extent of the "choice" he has.

Law: VATA 1994, Sch. 2, para. 4

10. "Waiver" of registration

10.1 Introduction

This section deals with cases where the entity is required to register for VAT, under the mandatory provisions, but can deploy various rules which allow it to agree with HMRC that registration is not necessary after all.

Before dealing with each case separately, there is a general health warning. Unless the entity applies to register and then actively requests waiver, it does not qualify for the waiver. It is clear from the law that failure to apply means that the waiver is not granted and the entity remains wrongly unregistered. If an entity wakes up to the fact that it ought to have applied, and probably would not have been registered on the information available at the time, then it can ask HMRC to consider the position retrospectively. Whilst HMRC are able (on their interpretation of the law at least) to agree retrospective waiver, they cannot look at evidence collected in the intervening period to inform their decision. This is because it would give late applicants an in-built advantage. HMRC must look at evidence that would have been available at the time the application ought to have been made. Thus, if there is no extant evidence from the time that the application should have been made this can cause difficulties.

There are two basic reasons for HMRC to grant a waiver:

- the supplier is only registerable because of zero-rated supplies; or
- the turnover threshold was exceeded only temporarily.

10.2 Zero-rated supplies

This allows HMRC to exempt the applicant from registration (upon receiving an application) as long as *any* supplies are zero-rated. This means that there can be positive rated supplies as well, and does not suggest that there needs to be any minimum proportion of zero-rated supplies.

This is reinforced by the fact that the exempted entity must inform HMRC within 30 days if "there is a material alteration in ... the proportion of taxable supplies ... that are zero-rated".

So, when will HMRC agree to the waiver? Basically, when satisfied that the entity would be in a net repayment position (input tax exceeds output tax) so that HMRC have the benefit of not reimbursing input tax. This is therefore not one of the most popular reliefs. It should also be noted that the business cannot change its mind retrospectively if it regrets the decision. It can only change its mind from a current date.

For non-established entities the equivalent provision requires all of the supplies to be zero-rated.

The same rule applies where an entity must register owing to making acquisitions of goods from other EU states and can demonstrate that the goods would be zero-rated in the UK.

Law: VATA 1994, Sch. 1, para. 14; Sch. 1A, para. 13

10.3 Turnover

If the business can show that, having exceeded the registration limits under the "look back" test, it will not exceed the de-registration limits (usually some £2,000 less than the registration limit) in the ensuing twelve months, HMRC may waive registration. This does not apply to the "look forward" test.

Any applicant for this waiver is required to monitor the position and notify HMRC if the position changes such that the turnover remains above the de-registration threshold. Even where the pattern is replicated by reality, the entity will again have to register if any later increase in turnover arises from general expansion.

There is an understandable temptation for applicants to try to "buy time" by requesting this waiver, but that is very risky. First, HMRC will probably need to have a clear and verifiable explanation as to why the turnover that gave rise to the obligation was an unusual "spike". Second, any evidence of insincerity is likely to be treated by HMRC with suspicion and could cause applicants who are guilty of little more than optimism (albeit, in business/commercial terms, more a case of pessimism) to be treated as plain dishonest.

Law: VATA 1994, Sch. 1, para. 1(3)

11. Groups of companies

11.1 The purposes of group registration

Group registration is a business facilitation measure which also reduces HMRC's administrative effort. It allows different entities to form one VAT registration and to submit common returns. This has the effect of aggregating both the sales and purchases of the grouped entities. It also allows supplies to be made between members of the VAT group without them being treated as supplies for VAT purposes (and accordingly no VAT is chargeable on them). All of the supplies of the group are deemed to be made by a nominated "representative member", but in practice, this simply means that all of the members of the group jointly make the supplies. The same is true of purchases by the group, which are deemed to have been made by the representative member. However, the characteristics of each member are preserved such that, if an entity qualifies for a particular VAT treatment (e.g. a charity qualifying for a purchase VAT relief) it does not lose this by becoming part of a VAT group.

In a nutshell, this means that several legal entities can be set up for particular activities, yet can be amalgamated to form a single VAT registration as though only one legal entity was used. This facilitates the setting up of "special purpose vehicles", without a change in the VAT position. It is particularly helpful where members of the group may be partly exempt, and therefore would incur irrecoverable VAT if sharing resources with fellow group members, were it not for the group registration facility.

Joint and several liability

There is, however, a significant health warning accompanying this. Members of a VAT group registration are all jointly and severally liable for the VAT liabilities of the group. This is a major impediment to forming VAT groups where, for instance, equity investors, or creditors, have an interest in a particular potential member of a group, and do not wish that entity to be exposed to the VAT debts of any of the others. Such companies are usually excluded from group registration under the requirements of the external investor or lender.

Law: VATA 1994, s. 43(1)

11.2 Who joins?

Before coming onto the specific criteria for qualifying to become a member of a group with other companies, there are some overarching points to make.

- Eligibility to join does not make it compulsory to join, and it is a matter of absolute choice by the taxpayer as to whether he becomes a member of a group of which he qualifies to be a member (subject to some rarely used anti-avoidance provisions to which we will come shortly).
- An entity does not have to be carrying on a business in order to join a VAT group registration, so to that extent the registration criteria are different from normal "single entity" registration criteria noted elsewhere. It is not possible for a single entity to register for VAT if it is not a business, whereas it could form part of a group VAT registration, as long as at least one member is in business. This is relevant to passive investment holding companies in particular.
- There is no need for any member of the group to make sufficient taxable supplies to exceed the VAT registration threshold in order to join it.
- It is possible to assemble a VAT group registration of several entities in such a fashion that the group itself does not make taxable supplies. However, this can only arise where supplies made within the group would be taxable if it were not for the group registration itself. Thus, for instance, a selection of entities whose activities are wholly exempt, but for the fact that they provide general services to each other, can form a VAT group registration, thus effectively negating the taxable supplies, even though the group itself makes solely exempt supplies. However, should these companies cease making supplies to each other, the criterion for group registration immediately

evaporates (unless it imports services or makes a "self-supply" of course).

11.3 Entity criteria

Before coming to what are called the "control criteria" it is worth making some comments about the nature of the entity and associated conditions.

- Under UK VAT group registration rules, only "bodies corporate" can be members of the VAT group registration. However, at the time of writing HMRC are in the process of reviewing the criteria for group membership in the wake of the CJEU's decision in *Larentia and Minerva*, in which the Court held that limitation to corporate bodies was not permitted under the directive.

- The limitation to corporate bodies is particularly unhelpful to unincorporated associations and to unincorporated charities. However, many unincorporated charities have incorporated their board of trustees (for various reasons, probably unrelated to VAT). Since an unincorporated charity is not deemed to exist as an entity in law, but exists only through its trustees (or trustee), the creation of a corporate trustee has the effect that the charity's activities are carried out by that corporate body. Admittedly, that is rarely applied in practice, and in such a situation HMRC usually accept that it is the unincorporated association that is registerable for VAT rather than a trustee corporate body itself. But there appear to be strong arguments in favour of HMRC allowing an unincorporated charity in this position to form a VAT group registration with its incorporated trading subsidiary company.

- The corporate body itself need not be UK incorporated, but it must have at the least a "fixed establishment" in the UK. A fixed establishment is an establishment with sufficient human and technical resources. Thus, for instance, a wholly owned foreign subsidiary of a UK company which has no establishment in the UK cannot form a VAT group registration with the UK company. This could be relevant when considering the treatment of reverse charges on

- imported services or the treatment of services supplied from the UK company to the overseas company.
- It is not possible for a company to be a member of more than one VAT group at the same time. Interestingly, it is perfectly possible for members of a single corporate group to form several different VAT group registrations. For instance, if there were eight companies in a corporate group, they could form four VAT group registrations which are parings of those eight companies. What cannot happen is that one company joins more than one group, even though it is actually individually qualified to join all of them. There must be a choice made between one or the other.
- A company that is a member of a VAT group may also be registered as part of a partnership if it is a partner in that partnership. The activities of the partnership are seen as separate from the activities of the company per se, the latter being covered solely by the group registration of which it is a member.
- Divisional registration (dealt with elsewhere in this book) cannot co-exist with group registration. If the benefits of divisional registration are particularly attractive, that particular company must register for VAT on its own.
- Tour operators, within the definition provided in the Tour Operators Margin Scheme legislation, cannot join a VAT group with another such tour operator if either has an overseas establishment.

Case: *Beteiligungsgesellschaft Larentia and Minerva mbH & Co. KG v Finanzamt Nordenham* C-108/14

11.4 Control criteria

11.4.1 Many-layered conditions

The control criteria (which are part of the range of issues under review following *Larentia and Minerva*) are complex, difficult, and potentially very troublesome. They split into two sets of conditions, one being general in nature, and the other relating to potential avoidance schemes, though an avoidance motive is not itself relevant in terms of engaging these special conditions. The best way to deal with the rules is to consider the basic conditions and, if fulfilled, then check the special conditions.

Case: *Beteiligungsgesellschaft Larentia and Minerva mbH & Co. KG v Finanzamt Nordenham* C-108/14

11.4.2 Basic conditions

The members of a potential group must be subject to control by one of the following:

- each other;
- a natural person (that is, an individual), or a body corporate, that controls all of the members; or
- two or more natural people who are carrying on a business in partnership, and who control all of the members.

Most of this is relatively simple. The most common situation in a VAT group is that one of the members of the group controls the others. But it is possible to set up a group between those that are controlled, without the controlling party being included in the group, and that is catered for under the second limb of the test above. Control of all of them by an individual means that the group members would exclude the controlling party, namely the individual. Even if the individual was carrying out a trade and was registered for VAT on his own account (as a sole proprietor), he cannot under the current rules form a group with the companies he controls.

But the most difficult of the provisions to interpret is the last, relating to partnerships. It is a dangerous provision because it is all too easy to conclude, erroneously, that any two people or entities, sharing control of relevant companies, fulfil this criterion. That is not true.

First, only a partnership between natural persons can have that effect. The implication is that any partnership which involves any non-natural person would not qualify. One might be able to argue that as long as the partnership includes two individuals, then it qualifies for that purpose even if it includes partners that are legal entities rather than natural entities. But that is probably a strained interpretation.

113

Then, there is also the need for the partnership to be carrying on a business. It should be borne in mind that this rule is supposed to deal both with English and Scottish partnerships (and in theory could include foreign partnerships). The definition of an English partnership would incorporate the carrying on of a business as a criterion of being such an entity. To that extent, the requirement that the partnership is carrying on a business seems almost superfluous, and it would have been sufficient simply to have stated that two or more individuals in partnership needed to control the members. But the fact that it is there emphasises the point that one cannot impute a partnership for these purposes unless the partnership is itself carrying on a business. Thus, it is not possible for people to gather together in some kind of non-business enterprise and treat themselves as controlling the entities which wish to form a VAT group. Consider, therefore, a situation where two or more people simply wish to invest in two companies and take dividends from them, without providing any business services to them or to anyone else. This is not a partnership and therefore the control criteria are not met unless one of those people themselves controls the entities to the exclusion of the other.

It is not uncommon for it to be thought that trustees of a charity can give rise to control of another entity (often a charity) where the majority of that entity's trustees are taken from the trustee pool of the other charity. This is not strictly correct, although HMRC have appeared on occasion to accept it.

Example

Charity A is an unincorporated charity, and two charities limited by guarantee are set up by Charity A for various other purposes. Charity A has twelve trustees, and sends four of these also to be trustees of Charity B Ltd. Charity B Ltd has three other trustees. Another four trustees of Charity A are sent also to be trustees of Charity C Ltd. Charity C has another three trustees.

It is clear that in each case the trustees derived from Charity A control both Charities B and C (leaving aside the further point that trustees owe a separate fiduciary duty to the charities of which they are trustee, and so cannot act in the interests of Charity A per se), even though Charities B and C have no common trustees between them.

> This creates the impression that Charity A controls B and C. But, for VAT group registration purposes this should not be accepted. This is because Charity A is not a body corporate, and it is not a partnership operating a business.

11.4.3 What is control?

The question of what is meant by control is determined by the criteria of *Companies Act* 2006, s. 1159 and Sch. 6. Where one company could be said to control another company, this can be tested directly by reference to the *Companies Act* criteria for being a "holding company". The principle also extends to an individual, or to individuals acting in a business partnership, by reference to the concept that they would have *Companies Act* control if they were themselves companies. However, in addition to the *Companies Act* criteria which will apply to almost all circumstances, it is possible for control criteria to be met where one body corporate is empowered by statute to control the activities of the other. Note, however, that the statutory power does not appear to extend to individuals.

This still begs the question as to what constitutes *Companies Act* control. This is in itself a legal question, but the most relevant test is that of whether the company (or the individual) can behave as a holding company, i.e. does it have more than 50% of the shareholding of the company in question, and (if so) does that give it practical control? Where control is exercised through a chain of companies, the question is effectively modified by reference to ultimate level of control taking into account the level of control each of the intermediary entities holds. Certain shares have lower voting power than others, and this needs to be taken into account. In simple terms, there needs to be an ability to control rather than merely a preponderance of shares or an ability simply to extract revenues. For this reason, preference shares are often not a clear indicator of "control".

11.4.4 Anti-avoidance control criteria

Introduction

To counter avoidance schemes which HMRC deemed to be an abuse, the *VAT (Groups: Eligibility) Order* 2004 was introduced with effect from 1 August 2004. We have now lived with these rules for nearly 15 years, and it appears that their practical effect has been to snuff out the "abuse" at which they were aimed, and thus they are easy to overlook because they are rarely engaged. But, as with most anti-avoidance provisions, one does not have to have an avoidance motive in order to fall foul of them, and there can be some exceptional situations where one might do so without realising it and thus invalidate the VAT group registration.

All of the following eligibility conditions are in addition to the basic control criteria conditions mentioned above. It is worth noting that they are clearly separate because although provision is made in primary legislation for such extra rules, the rules themselves arise in secondary legislation (a statutory instrument), and are therefore qualitatively different from the basic control criteria (though that does not mean that they are any weaker in their application to taxpayers). The rules apply according to the following provisions which represent "hurdles" that can be considered in turn.

Turnover threshold

The *VAT (Groups: Eligibility) Order* rules only apply where either:

- the value of the proposed VAT group's supplies in the year then ending have exceeded £10m; or
- there are reasonable grounds for believing that the value of the proposed group's supplies in the year then commencing will exceed £10m.

Interestingly, the calculation requires one to treat the proposed group as though it were already a group and thus measure its turnover. The supplies in question do not appear to be taxable supplies, so can include exempt and outside scope supplies, which of course may be very relevant in terms of the desirable effect of VAT grouping. Specifically, where a group registration already exists, and there is a proposal to add a member, it is the aggregate of the proposed member and the existing group which needs to be reviewed in the light of this threshold.

Management control

Subject to all of the conditions, VAT group registration is denied where:

- the company (which is under consideration) is not wholly owned by the person that controls all of the other members of the group;
- it is managed, whether directly or indirectly, by a third party, where that third party is carrying out a management business of some kind; or
- it is the sole general partner of a limited partnership (referring to the *Limited Partnership Act* 1907).

However, there is no such limitation applicable to charities, or to bodies corporate which only act as trustee for a pension scheme.

Relevant activity

If the above pertain, disqualification potentially applies where there is a "relevant activity". This is defined as one where:

- the company in question supplies goods or services to one or more other members of the target group;
- the supplies are not incidental to its business activity (that is, it is a core purpose of that company's activities);
- at least one of the supplies would be chargeable at a positive rate of VAT; and
- the group as a whole was, prior to the potential accession of the company in question, unable to reclaim all of its input tax.

Benefits condition

If the above pertain, disqualification applies where the company in question would pay out more than 50% of its profits to the third party in question. This includes:

- profits (whether or not distributed);
- charges for managing the business (including supplies of staff); and
- charges by which any other charges made to the body in question exceed the open market value of the goods and services concerned (that is, a profit overage).

From this it can be seen that the intention is not to allow group registration where the majority of the financial benefit of running the company will devolve to third parties rather than to the true beneficial owners of the group (so to speak).

Consolidated accounts condition

Even where the benefits rule does not trigger disqualification, this rule may do so instead. If the accounts of the company would (or ought to) be consolidated with the accounts of the group which it seeks to join, then it cannot join the group if all but one of the preceding tests are failed. The excepted test is the benefits rule. Even if that is passed, the company would still be unable to join the group.

HMRC flow chart

A useful flow chart shows HMRC's interpretation of these rules at page VGROUPS03750 of the manuals.

It can be seen from all of this that it is unlikely to catch those without an avoidance motive, and is particularly aimed at large concerns (by reference to the £10m turnover criterion). As with many provisions of this nature, the threshold at which it becomes applicable has not been upgraded for inflation, and seems unlikely to be revisited. This presents a constant "ratchet" which makes its impact wider as time goes by.

Law: SI 2004/1931

11.5 Specific HMRC powers

Whilst, in fundamental terms, the choice of whether a group registration should exist between companies that qualify is one for the companies and not for HMRC, HMRC are granted a power under the legislation to refuse an application to register companies as a group, or to refuse accession of any particular company to an existing VAT group. If they wish to do so, HMRC must demonstrate that it is "for the protection of the revenue" (VATA 1994, s. 43B(5), (6)). However, the general VAT efficiencies that arise in the course of VAT group registration would not be regarded as threatening HMRC's revenues, and cannot be considered by them as a basis for refusing group registration. It is therefore rare for group registration to be refused, but HMRC have a power to do so in any situation where they do not accept that the circumstances are normal. If they make such a decision, it is appealable to the VAT tribunals, but only on a "supervisory basis", which means that the VAT tribunal may only consider whether HMRC's decision is reasonable rather than whether the tribunal would have made the same negative decision (VATA 1994, s. 84(4C)).

The way in which this is handled is that HMRC will provisionally accept a VAT group registration and must notify the applicants within 15 days of having received the VAT group application of the provisional acceptance, but then are allowed a total of 90 days in which to reverse that decision. Thus, they have 90 days from the date of receipt of the application to determine whether they will confirm that the group registration exists. If they decide not to confirm that it exists, then it will be deemed never to have existed, rather than to be disbanded at the point at which they make their decision. Once the 90 day "cooling off" window has passed, the VAT group is deemed to exist. HMRC have certain powers to override the effects of the group that they have allowed, and these are dealt with below. Otherwise, the group is then deemed to exist.

This gives rise to the common point that a VAT group registration will invariably be confirmed initially as a provisional registration but with a rather threatening comment that further investigations are being carried out into the application which may cause it to be rejected. However, experience suggests that it is rarely followed up, and it is not clear to what extent the investigations even take place beyond further scrutiny of the information on the face of the application form. The matter is left to drop and there is no further confirmation issued by HMRC to the effect that the investigations prove satisfactory. This can be disconcerting to applicants who are not aware of this procedural approach.

It follows that where taxpayers are relying upon being part of a valid VAT group registration to avoid excessive VAT cost, and need to form a new VAT group registration to achieve this, or add a company to an existing group, it is wise to predict the situation far in advance, at least 90 days before it will arise, so that the cooling off period will have passed before the relevant transactions take place. If that does not happen, then the transactions may take place during a period when, ostensibly, the group registration existed, but not in a period where one could be certain that it will be deemed to have existed. Thus the supply which needed, for the sake of VAT efficiency, to be carried out between the two parties in the same VAT group, may retrospectively be subject to VAT if HMRC withdraw their approval within the cooling off period.

11.6 Further anti-avoidance provisions

VATA 1994, Sch. 9A includes some extremely difficult provisions which give HMRC powers to direct the VAT group be deemed non-applicable in so far as intra-group supplies are concerned. It is the writer's experience that the powers in Sch. 9A are never or hardly ever deployed by HMRC. To that extent, they have fulfilled the desired consequence of deterrence.

These provisions arose as a result of companies using the timing of VAT group registration to achieve significant input tax savings which were not thought by HMRC to be justifiable (and, in fairness, they were not). Typically this involved the setting up of a captive company of a heavily partly exempt group of traders (for example, in the insurance industry) to purchase assets on the basis of making onward supplies to the group companies. The new company was group registered with the operational companies, charged a high proportion of the price to them when still a group member, then "de-grouped" just before it reclaimed input VAT, and charged a small amount of VAT on the small balancing payment. This heavily reduced the output tax which would not have been recoverable by the partly exempt companies, without (supposedly) reducing input tax recovery.

Admittedly, this scheme did not work (the Courts refused to uphold it). But this convinced HMRC that further powers were needed, in addition to those denying group registration (as above), which therefore led to Sch. 9A. This provision goes further and provides specific powers.

The provisions of Sch. 9A do not necessarily change the fact of whether or not members of a group remain as members or become members, but the impact of the provisions is almost as if that were the case, so it is worth mentioning the provisions in overview.

The issue with giving HMRC a power to refuse a group registration application "for the protection of the revenue" is that they cannot really be expected to spot situations where their revenue is under threat. This means that they need a back-up, which is what Sch. 9A provides. It allows HMRC to deem that two group members are not grouped in respect of certain abusive transactions. Those transactions are as described above, namely where a sum of input tax has been claimed but, by means of the timing of accession or departure to and from a group, only a small proportion of the value of the input tax is ever returned as output tax. This is described in Schedule 9A as a supply at an "undervalue". Where that exists, and, critically, where there is no commercial purpose which gave rise to the situation, HMRC are able to issue a direction that the intra-group supply be treated as a self supply at full value, thus giving rise to irrecoverable input tax. This is dealt with by way of an assessment for:

- the net of the deemed output tax; minus
- the related input tax that would be allowed to the group had the grouping that existed not been in place.

In a more general way HMRC can deem the group not to have been effectual between certain dates, so this has a similar effect to its being disbanded.

HMRC can also deem that two companies that would qualify to choose to be group registered are actually to be taken to be registered as a group (thus snuffing out a taxable supply between the entities that might have given rise to input tax recovery).

This power has retrospective application of six years, and so can be used to catch historic transactions on a "discovery" basis.

It should be noted that, whilst the failed scheme that inspired HMRC to introduce Sch. 9A was an "exit scheme" (the company leaves the group after charging a large fee) it is intended by HMRC to protect against an "entry scheme" (the input tax is claimed before joining a group and then charging most of the consideration within the group). That said, entry schemes must be easier for them to spot than exit schemes.

Law: VATA 1994, Sch. 9A

11.7 Timing of the application

As a working rule, you cannot form a group, or change its composition, retrospectively. Section 43B (4) puts it this way:

"an application ... shall ... be taken to be granted with effect from –

(a) the day on which the application is received by the Commissioners, or

(b) such earlier or later time as the Commissioners may allow."

The first thing to note is the general position that the date will be that on which the application is received by HMRC. One assumes that electronic application is instant so the day it is sent is also the day it is received. But postal application entails delay, and you cannot automatically backdate to the date you sent the application.

However, HMRC have a power to allow backdating. There is nothing more in the legislation than as given above, so one might imagine that the decision to allow backdating would depend on such issues as whether it would prejudice HMRC as compared with the position had they received the application "on time" and what level of adverse impact any decision not to backdate has on the applicant. But that is not how HMRC see the position at all. They take the following view:

"Can my application be backdated?

Yes, but only up to 30 days prior to your application being received by us and only if it corresponds to the commencement of the current accounting period of:

- the existing VAT group; or
- any of the companies forming, joining or leaving the VAT group.

So, if the commencement of the current accounting period is less than 30 days prior to your application being received by us, the maximum period of retrospection will be the beginning of that accounting period.

Can I backdate my application for more than 30 days?

Only in exceptional circumstances, Exceptional circumstances include:

- if we lose your application and you can supply details of your original application and your attempts to follow it up; or
- if the delay was caused by lack of action on our part.

These examples are not exhaustive. However, we would not consider a failure to apply for grouping earlier because of ignorance or a misunderstanding on your part to be in itself an 'exceptional circumstance'. Neither would we consider a situation where you simply find that in hindsight you could have arranged things to better effect if you had chosen to group earlier."

The degree of retrospection offered is verging on the immaterial. If one wants a greater level of retrospection, they say it can only arise if it is their error. This is very strange since, naturally, one would expect them not to hold their own errors against an applicant. The law cannot be intended to be restricted to cases of official error. This means that, bar the 30 day rule, HMRC effectively consider that there is no retrospection allowable. This writer would argue that HMRC should not approach a legal power by saying that they have carte blanche not to apply it, but should rather consider each request on its merits. In practice HMRC simply refer to the above extract in their Notice. Whilst this has been challenged in tribunal cases, the result is that HMRC need only point to a cost to them of backdating in order to justify refusing it, which is not the same as saying that their position is prejudiced as compared with a more timely application. This "rule" is in urgent need of reconsideration.

It is clear also that an applicant can make an application in good time to create a group (or change it) from a future date. One imagines that this would only tend to apply so as to allow a change to occur from the next VAT accounting period. In practice that is very common. The date of receipt is rarely the most logical date for the change. But applicants also ought to consider whether the change could be from the beginning of the next VAT year (not merely VAT return period). Where an entity is partly exempt HMRC take the view that a new group truncates the existing partial exemption year, which can have unintended consequences. Even a change to an existing group can affect partial exemption annual adjustment calculations in ways that are all too easy to overlook.

11.8 Phantom groups

The sin that dare not speak its name is the assumed group registration that does not exist or where an entity is included in the returns for a group when it is not actually a member. This is probably more common than anyone realises. Group applications can be overlooked. In cases where there is no rational reason why the group application would be refused, HMRC cannot be thought to have lost out. But it presents a severe compliance issue, for the following reasons:

- the input tax claimed on the phantom member is invalid;
- the supplies made within the group and deemed not to be supplies for VAT purposes were in fact taxable supplies and thus are under declared;
- partial exemption calculations include turnover (or other units of measurement) which did not arise from a genuine group member, thus rendering the calculations invalid;
- one or more entities has failed to register at the correct time and is subject to penalties on the tax that was not properly declared;
- the phantom members are not protected by the four year cap;
- various rules arising from the assumed scale of the operation may have been invalidated by the omission (e.g. monthly payments on account).

The obvious solution, absent anything exceptional, would be for HMRC silently to allow the phantom member to be admitted from a date it became a *de facto* member, but there is no suggestion that HMRC will in fact do this. It is not unknown for them to follow the example of Admiral Lord Nelson and put a blind eye to the telescope rather than trying to unpick the mess, but they then retain the right to create trouble, which is unfortunate and, again, ought to be reviewed.

11.9 Leaving the group

There are three basic situations here:

- a member wishes to leave a group of which he continues to qualify to be a member;
- a member no longer qualifies to be a member and thus ought to leave;
- HMRC exercise a power of direct removal of a member

The rules for leaving are similar to the rules for joining in that, where HMRC receive an application, they will disband the group from the date of receipt of the application, unless they decide that an earlier or later date is acceptable. Thus, one can apply for a change from a logical date in the near future and HMRC will usually grant that request.

The position arising where an entity no longer qualifies to be a member is more complex. It is often assumed (with some reason) that once the control criteria are no longer met, the membership ceases by process of law, and all that is required is that HMRC are told of the fact and adjust the register accordingly. This is not true. VATA 1994, s. 43C clearly provides that HMRC can specify a date, in a notice, from which the adjustment to the membership of the group applies. HMRC must issue a notice once they become aware that the criteria are not met. The date specified in the notice may be earlier than the date the notice is actually issued, but this date cannot be earlier than the date on which the control criteria were no longer met (subject to a further power mentioned below).

The meaning is clear. It is that HMRC can cause a group to carry on beyond the date of the criteria being met. In practice they would only do this to counter avoidance arising from manipulation of the date of exit. But consideration needs to be given to the impact of this if reliance is being placed on a taxation outcome arising from automatic de-grouping merely by changing (say) the shareholding in a company. That on its own is not enough. Application needs to be made timeously as well. Indeed, even with timely application, HMRC have powers to hang fire and delay de-grouping.

Finally, HMRC do have a nuclear option of de-grouping an entity or disbanding a group from a current date "for the protection of the revenue". This works hand in hand with the more invasive Sch. 9A powers alluded to above.

Law: VATA 1994, s. 43C

12. Divisional registration

Now rarely used, this facility used to be important in the days of self-accounting divisions where the book keeping arrangements did not allow rapid consolidation of results. This is now rare, so the rules are all but academic. The facility is supposed to be used purely to aid administrative compliance and there is no clear opportunity to use it to reduce liabilities or affect cash flow.

Divisions can arise from geographical separation or complete business separation (such as a vertically integrated business or a heavily diversified business).

In simple terms the facility allows you to opt to submit a separate VAT return for each individual operating division within one single entity, as if they were separate registrations. However the following points apply:

- this is only allowed if HMRC are satisfied that the facility is needed because the accounting system is sufficiently separate and that not to allow it will place strain on the business's administrative system;
- supplies between divisions of the same entity remain a "non-event" for VAT purposes;
- the applicant is fully taxable (does not have to apportion its input tax);
- the return "stagger" (the quarters on which returns are due) is the same for all divisions;
- it is not possible for a company that is using divisional registration also to be part of a VAT group;
- by definition, inception of divisional registration only occurs from a current date;
- all divisions of the entity must be registered.

Application for divisional registration is made by letter. A divisionally registered company will have a different VAT number per division (which could prove puzzling to customers if they do business with more than one division).

Law: VATA 1994, s. 46

13. De-registering from VAT

13.1 Introduction

The main topic of this book is "registration", but de-registration is nonetheless an aspect. There are three main issues:

- When may I voluntarily de-register?
- When must I de-register?
- What are the consequences of de-registering in either case?

13.2 Voluntary de-registration

13.2.1 General rules

There is a "de-registration threshold" (which is actually the exception from registration figure), which has traditionally "tracked" the registration threshold at £2k less (though there is no obvious reason why it should be this figure). The general approach is that once an entity's turnover is below that threshold the entity need no longer be registered until and unless it exceeds the registration thresholds.

The legislation specifically allows HMRC to entertain de-registration where the entity satisfies HMRC that its taxable turnover in the ensuing year will be below the prevailing "de-registration threshold"[1]. Nothing more is said about the standard of proof needed and whether HMRC can exercise any discretion (on its own behalf) in any particular circumstances. It seems reasonable, at least, that a business which shows an explicable reduction to less than the de-registration threshold for a period of a whole year ought to be accepted as having made its case for de-registration, but there is no test that sets this in stone. Rather, even if the entity has not traded for a year at below the threshold, it can still apply on the basis of a trend that suggests it will do so in the forthcoming year, though that, naturally, would be less persuasive.

---

[1] The legislation refers to the entity no longer breaching the registration threshold, though in practice there is not likely to be a meaningful difference.

It is worth noting that the threshold is not necessarily based on the registered person's Box 6 turnover figure in his VAT return. That net taxable figure does not accurately represent the value of taxable supplies to final consumers that would arise if the entity were not registered. That is because the VAT element has been removed. This would become part of the taxable turnover if the business was no longer registered (assuming "shop prices" remained unchanged by de-registering). It is that "gross turnover" that remains relevant when considering the value of supplies for de-registration. The following example illustrates this.

Example

Hacker Ltd's retail turnover has reduced to £75,000 per year according to the Box 6 figure in the VAT return (which is below the threshold at the time of writing). The director decides to de-register. However this £75,000 turnover represents a till take of £90,000 (£75k x 120% – assuming a VAT rate of 20%). This means that the company will amass a taxable turnover of £90,000 within the year. If, say, the registration limit is £85,000, it will cross the threshold within the year. The company should not be allowed to de-register on the basis of a predicted turnover at that level, and should not apply to do so.

The legislation specifically precludes de-registration arising from a reduction in turnover created by a closure of the business for 30 days or more. This probably addresses the risk of temporal fragmentation (that is, seeking to put the sales from a portion of the year into a second entity in order to keep both entities below the registration threshold). The impact on a business that once was year-round but later becomes seasonal is not catered for explicitly. However, it would be reasonable to presume that a genuine move to more seasonal trade (even if at the choice of the proprietor) would be treated sympathetically as not necessarily falling into this category.

As with the registration rules, prospective sales of capital goods are not treated as turnover unless they involve positive rated land, but in these cases the impact of the exit charge for de-registering would in any case create a disincentive to de-registering (discussed below).

It should be borne in mind that all of the deemed supplies (such as reverse charge services) and the issues relating to value of consideration (such as barter transactions), which are explored in detail elsewhere in this book, apply equally here. Such transactions represent "turnover" for these purposes and should not be overlooked.

Law: VATA 1994, Sch. 1, para. 11-13

13.2.2 Acquisition

Similar rights to de-register apply (but with relevant modifications) where the reason to be registered arises from acquisition of goods from the EU or from the distance selling rules.

For acquisitions, there is no specific de-registration threshold. Rather, the right to be de-registered is based on simply falling below the registration threshold. In this case the track record of the prior year does provide objective conditions for de-registering. However, the applicable year is the calendar year, not any rolling twelve month period. Interestingly, the "look forward" test makes an appearance here in that the registration will not be cancelled if there are grounds for believing that acquisitions in excess of the threshold will arise within the ensuing thirty days. This acts as a backstop if the objective evidence of the prior year's acquisitions would lead automatically to a right to de-register. However, it is fairly unlikely that an entity in that position would predict a major acquisition in the next thirty days, though that is technically possible.

In addition, the entity can apply to de-register on the basis that acquisitions in the ensuing calendar year will fall below the registration threshold.

All of this is modified if the entity had applied voluntarily to register under the acquisitions banner and then decides to de-register voluntarily. This could easily happen where a business decided that it was better to incur UK VAT (presumably because the rate was lower than the VAT rate in the EU state from which the goods travelled) but later wished to switch to incurring VAT at the rate of the EU state from which the goods came (presumably where the UK rate becomes uncompetitive). To avoid short term opt-in/opt-out behaviour, the de-registration in such cases cannot occur before 1

January in the year following the second anniversary of the original registration. Thus, if an entity chooses to register for acquisitions and has no other basis to be able to choose to be VAT registered (which implies that it makes solely exempt supplies of course) it cannot change its mind for at least two years, and perhaps longer. That said, even a small line of taxable activities (or activities that would be taxable if carried on in the UK) will rescue the entity from this restriction.

Law: VATA 1994, Sch. 3, para. 5-7

13.2.3 Distance selling

The same applies in this situation. An entity that chooses to register for distance selling when it was not obliged to do so cannot switch back to home-country rates of VAT until 1 January after the second complete year of being registered. Thus if a Swedish company (say) chooses to register for UK VAT under distance selling, to benefit from the favourable UK VAT rate, and (in the unlikely event) Sweden's rate goes lower than the UK's, the entity cannot simply de-register unless it has been registered for at least two years.

Law: VATA 1994, Sch. 2, para. 6-7

13.2.4 Registration arising from sale of goods on which VAT claimed

This arises from the unusual cause of registration, namely selling goods on which an entity reclaimed VAT under overseas business provisions covered at **2.5.3**. Basically, HMRC will agree to de-register the entity once it has "ceased to make relevant supplies".

Law: VATA 1994, Sch. 3A, para. 6

13.3 Compulsory de-registration

This arises where the registered entity no longer has the intention to make taxable supplies or to make supplies that are deemed to be "taxable" for voluntary registration purposes. Once that intention ceases the entity must notify HMRC within 30 days and HMRC will then de-register the entity from that date or any later date agreed.

No definition is provided as to what entails an intention to make taxable (or quasi taxable) supplies (or more accurately, a lack of such intention). However it is reasonable to assume that there must be something more than a mere wish or whim to make such supplies at some point, but rather a demonstrable intention which is specific enough not to be a mere hope. HMRC may well seek evidence of intention along similar lines to that requested when considering a voluntary registration application. But, as with voluntary registration, there is no compulsion to make the supplies themselves if the intention is frustrated and no supplies actually transpire.

Clearly, a break in a business which arises in circumstances where there is a real desire to restart the business (e.g. a restaurant is shut down due to health and safety issues but there is an intention to clear the problem and get it opened again) is not the same as the position of an entity which shuts down one business but hopes to start something completely different. HMRC will take more persuading by an entity which is making a significant change, and will probably call for evidence of the new intention.

However, the scale of the supplies to be made is not in itself a relevant factor. The taxable supplies can be maintained at a very low level, thereby avoiding compulsory de-registration as long as the activity does amount to a business. It is more likely that HMRC will accept that an entity that has operated a business-like activity in the past will operate a business in the future.

This begs two questions: how would HMRC know that the business had (arguably) ceased, and why would it matter?

First, HMRC would only know when supplies ceased to be made, probably for two or three quarters in a row. Whilst the registered entity is required to notify any cessation within 30 days, as long as no intention to make taxable supplies subsists, any such continuing intention makes that irrelevant and HMRC will only engage with the point if the activity appears to cease.

HMRC do, however, have reason to care, quite apart from the fact that the legislation requires them to care. One reason is the cost of keeping dormant businesses on the register (though this must now be much lower since electronic filing became compulsory). A second is the fact that HMRC can collect tax in the process of de-registration of an entity.

131

13.4 Disadvantages of de-registering

Most of the disadvantages of de-registering are covered in **Chapter 1**, which deals with the disadvantages of not being registered in the first place, but there is a distinct disadvantage to de-registering which ought to be recognised before allowing a situation to arise where de-registration is necessary. This is that any assets on hand are deemed to be supplied at open market value, and the VAT on that value is payable to HMRC if it would be more than £1,000. (But note than not all assets will be subject to VAT, as some may be zero-rated. Others may only be subject to VAT on the margin between acquisition value and the current open market value, if they were acquired under the second hand margin scheme).

The above rule does not apply if there was VAT charged to the entity upon acquiring the goods and it could reclaim none of that VAT. But if it did reclaim it, or if it reclaimed any proportion (however small), or it did not pay VAT on it, then it owes the VAT. Furthermore, as this is not a supply to any other party, there is nobody to claim back the VAT.

Clearly it is better to sell the goods for scrap than to allow a case whereby this "exit charge" arises. Furthermore, the open market value is in effect the price for which you could buy the goods in that condition on the open market at the time. Where rapidly depreciating goods are concerned it is better to delay de-registration to a date when that value is much reduced than to pay a high exit charge only to watch the market value deteriorate after having paid VAT on a high value.

14. Penalties

14.1 Introduction

This book is about getting VAT registration right rather than dealing with the consequences of failing to do so. The rules relating to penalties can also change somewhat independently of the specific rules about VAT registration. For that reason, reference should be made as necessary to the specific VAT penalties rules. Nevertheless, the following is a brief guide that applies at the time of writing and that provides some pointers.

The current penalties for failure to register on time apply as a percentage to the net payable tax.

14.2 Honest error

For honest omission to register, the penalty can be as high as 30%. It may be possible to escape the penalty by reference to a "reasonable excuse". Jurisprudence relating to "reasonable excuse" has built up in abundance over the years, but a mere oversight will not qualify as such.

By way of examples, it may be possible to argue that there was a reasonable excuse where there has been a tricky decision regarding:

- VAT liability as such (whether exempt or taxable);
- whether an activity amounts to a business;
- whether a barter arises;
- whether an imported service falls within the reverse charge; or
- anything else which presents challenges of interpretation beyond the application of the registration rules *per se*.

However, even here there is potential for difficulty if the entity saw an issue that could have triggered the thought of VAT but failed to canvass the point with HMRC or to take professional advice. For instance, if a barter is shown as such in the statutory accounts, or a payment is shown as having been made in the internal accounting records, but this did not trigger the response that the related VAT position ought to be considered, it is not going to be easy to establish a reasonable excuse. Nor is reliance on a third party in itself sufficient, though there is case law which indicates a boundary to this principle.

Mitigation

However, HMRC have the power to mitigate all the way down to zero in accordance with the "behaviours" of the taxpayer. They can (though they are not required to) set the rate at 0% for an unprompted disclosure as long as the delay is no more than 12 months, or 10% for a longer delay. An "unprompted" disclosure is one made when HMRC were not known by the entity or its advisers to be looking into the situation or where there was no reason for the entity to think that it was being looked into or about to be looked into. If the disclosure was "prompted", then the reduction can be to 10% if the delay is within 12 months, or 20% otherwise. The likelihood of achieving these reductions depends on the level of co-operation with HMRC that the entity provides after the disclosure has been made.

14.3 Dishonest error

For dishonest failure to register the penalties are much higher. Dishonest failure arises where it is not a mistake and where the directors (or perhaps one of them), or persons of equivalent status, knew that VAT registration was required but deliberately failed to contact HMRC. It is possible to have done this deliberately at one stage and then repent of the dishonesty later, and accordingly bring the point to HMRC's attention. That remains a dishonest failure to register, as the earlier dishonesty is not expunged by the later repentance, though the latter can help to reduce the penalties that apply.

There are two kinds of dishonesty, one that involves no cover up, and one where steps are taken to cover the tracks. The penalty regime recognises the different gravity of the two. The unconcealed dishonesty merits a maximum penalty of 70% (mitigable to some degree depending on disclosure and "behaviour") and the concealed dishonesty merits a maximum of 100%. An example of concealed dishonesty is where false documents are generated to seek to "prove" that registration was unnecessary and other forms of deliberate false accounting. Unconcealed dishonesty would be simply deliberately missing the deadline to register but doing nothing else to cover the position (such that all other aspects of the business are left as they would have been had there been no intention to cheat HMRC).

14.4 Pre April 2010 penalties

To the extent that the default goes back several years, there are different penalty rules which may be engaged in regard to tax from that period. However, this again is a subject of its own and the following is a brief overview.

All failure to register was subject to penalty unless the entity could demonstrate "reasonable excuse". However, the penalty was more lenient ranging from 5% to 15% (via 10%) depending on whether one was up to nine months late, up to 18 months late, or more than 18 months late.

Dishonesty was dealt with in a similar manner to today, but there was not a clear distinction between concealed and unconcealed dishonesty.

14.5 Reasonable excuse case

Whilst a review of the reasonable excuse case law is beyond the scope of a book about compliance with registration rules (there being around 100 decisions), the most amusing and astonishing case on the subject cannot be passed over. *Jenkinson* (an old case from 1988) involved a businessman who met a man on his regular train commute and was given to believe that the latter was an accountant who would handle VAT registration for him. The man was only ever encountered on the train, and he did not ask for any payment for his services. In due course the man gave the appellant a "VAT number". The appellant realised, however, that he had not received a return to complete and so contacted HMRC. He was told that the number was bogus.

The tribunal accepted the contention that there was a reasonable excuse because the appellant had not merely placed reliance on a third party but had taken steps to ensure that he did receive the evidence of having been registered. He could not be blamed for having been the victim of a con trick. This is a clear precedent for the defence of having been conned, though how likely these precise circumstances would be accepted in our more sceptical era the reader can judge for himself.

Law: FA 2008, s. 123 and Sch. 41

Case: *Keith Edward Jenkinson v C&E Commrs* [1988] VATTR 45

14.6 Security payment

Though not a penalty associated with late registration, there are provisions that enable HMRC to require a taxpayer to pay an amount of security against the possible risk of defaulting on his VAT liabilities. They often demand this at the time of registering an entity. This risk is determined by looking at the compliance history of previous businesses run by partners or directors of the entity. The security must be deposited as a condition of being allowed to make supplies. It is illegal to trade without paying the security.

15. Completing the forms

15.1 Introduction

The forms themselves vary from time to time and it is not the intention here to provide a blow by blow account of how to complete them. In any case, HMRC's published guidance on completing the forms is fairly comprehensive. However, the following practical points arise.

15.2 Applicable forms

At the time of writing these were:

VAT 1	Basic application form
VAT 1A	For distance selling
VAT 1B	For acquisitions
VAT 1C	For selling goods where VAT claimed by overseas entity
VAT 2	Lists partners in a partnership
VAT 5L	Supplementary information where making land supplies
VAT 50 & VAT 51	For forming or changing a group registration
VAT 1614 (series)	Option to tax form often submitted with VAT 1
VAT 7	To cancel registration
Letter	This is the only way to apply for divisional registration
VAT 68	To transfer the existing registration number under a TOGC (not advised)

These forms can generally be submitted online but, at the time of writing, could also be printed off and submitted by post. Some can be printed and completed manually, whereas others have to be completed on the computer but can then be printed off for physical submission.

15.3 Information with application

All information requested on the forms is important but it is worth considering the following in particular:

- The VAT 1 form is ambiguous over whether the incorporation details of foreign registered companies need to be included. In practice HMRC want to see these, so they are worth including.

- HMRC are very reluctant to register any business that does not have a bank account. They will also commonly query accounts of which the name does not match the entity's name or trading name, even where the name does match that of a parent or associated company. It seems that this is to do with anti-money laundering formalities.

- The details of current and recent past business involvement of all directors/partners need to be provided (as a compliance check) and this can be irksome where there are many of these. This also applies to charity trustees. Some entities find it excessively difficult to provide a complete list, but not doing so is a compliance failure and should not be contemplated on a deliberate or indolent basis. Where there is genuine doubt or difficulty this ought to be pointed out to HMRC in a covering letter or attachment.

- The details of the signatory, such as NI number (or overseas equivalent) and home address (including any recent previous address) appear invasive in nature, but, again, are part of HMRC's method of spotting fraud and cannot be omitted in the interests of personal privacy.

- Take care in choosing the date from which the registration is to commence as it is extremely difficult to obtain further backdating if, at a later date, you realise that the date you chose (or allowed to apply by default) does not cover retrospective claims sufficiently. This is easily overlooked.

15.4 Partnership application

The VAT 2 form lists all partners in a traditional (1890 Act and Scottish equivalent) partnership. It is not merely required when the partnership first registers but ought to be used to update the records of HMRC whenever a change in the partners of a business occurs. This, however, may be honoured more in the breach than in the observance. It is particularly important to inform HMRC when a partner retires from a partnership as HMRC otherwise take the view that the individual remains jointly and severally liable for the VAT debts of the partnership (though whether they take that point in most practical situations must be open to doubt). The best way to achieve this is to submit a revised VAT 2 on any change in the partners as this automatically updates HMRC's records. However, this is not straightforward where the retiring partner has no authority to apply on behalf of the partnership he has just left, so in that case there seems little alternative but to submit a letter or email to HMRC.

In practice HMRC accept notification of such matters in writing from any partner of the firm.

Form VAT 2 is also used where HMRC deem there to be a partnership even where none in fact exists. This is typically the case where trustees of an unincorporated charitable association are concerned or where joint land owners come together to exploit jointly held land. This is not a particularly satisfactory situation, since it requires people to sign up to a statement that they form a partnership, when they do not. However, there appears to be little choice in the matter.

The VAT 2 form needs to be signed by all of the listed partners (or quasi-partners) and this is a major administrative burden. Indeed, the VAT 2 seems to be a very old fashioned means of information gathering and alternative formats ought to be considered by HMRC.

15.5 Group application

This requires submission of a VAT 1, VAT 50, and VAT 51 (or more than one of these) where a new group is being set up. The VAT 1 is dispensed with when the intention is merely to add or remove members from the group. It is strange that there are three forms (or two for amendments) when one would have thought that one would do, but that seems to be based on history.

There are several points that are only tangentially related to the forms themselves.

First, creating a new group gives rise to a new VAT registration number and this can be inconvenient and may lead to error where the business fails to notice the new number and continues to print the old defunct number on invoices (though HMRC have allowed "old stocks" of pre-printed invoices to be used up before re-printing with the new number but this has long since been irrelevant to all but the most antiquated business operations).

It is HMRC's policy to view a new group as a new "taxable person" for the purposes of partial exemption, which means that the creation of a new group registration midway through a tax year can give rise to significant impact on the annual partial exemption calculation. It is not clear that HMRC are correct in taking this view, but, all other things considered, it may be better to delay the start date of a new group until the beginning of a tax year. The same general point applies to any partly exempt entity which is to be brought into a group registration.

15.6 Isle of Man

There is a separate register for Isle of Man (IoM) entities, or non-IoM entities which only make supplies in the IoM. With that exception, the registration rules are the same and the forms are similar. If an entity is registered for VAT in the UK then it need not register in the IoM and vice versa. Any transactions carried out in both the IoM and the UK must be reflected in the IoM return (or, as the case may be, in the UK return). IoM companies can form a group registration with UK companies and that group can be "held" on either the IoM or UK registers. As is well known, the IoM is treated as though it were in the UK in terms of the treatment of transactions with it.

15.7 Transferring the old VAT number

If the VAT 68 form is completed in the case of a TOGC, the old entity's VAT number can (with its agreement) be transferred to the new entity. This is discussed at **2.4.8**, and is generally better avoided.

16. The flat rate scheme

16.1 Introduction

The flat rate scheme for VAT is not part of the registration scenario *per se*, but it is likely to be one of the first considerations facing an adviser in regard to a newly registered or registerable business, and is included in this book for that reason.

This chapter considers the nature of the scheme and whether it is beneficial, the qualification for joining it, the process for joining and leaving it, and the method of accounting for VAT if one is a member. It is not, however, intended to replicate the large body of official information in Notice 733, which should be the first port of call for all potential users or applicants.

16.2 The purpose of the scheme

The stated purpose of the flat rate scheme is to reduce the accounting burdens on business by omitting (for the most part) input tax accounting (VAT on purchases) and relying on a fixed but lower effective rate of VAT to be declared on the sales to offset the loss of input tax.

The supplier may issue tax invoices showing VAT at the relevant standard rate, and the customer may reclaim the full VAT charged, without compromising the supplier's ability to use the lower rate of effective VAT charge inherent in the scheme's terms and conditions.

That said, as the scheme works on flat rates that are pre-determined, this has the effect of often taking the net VAT liability lower than would apply if the normal system of full inputs and outputs accounting was followed. Changes from April 2017 have altered that position in many cases. But it remains possible, in some instances, that it is financially advantageous to operate this scheme. Whilst the opposite can be true, it is rare than anyone wittingly uses the scheme when the consequence is that they will pay more. It is possible, therefore, that the original architects of this scheme intended it to have a mild financial effect to ease transition from being un-registered to being registered, but this is likely to be at best a limited impact, and is no longer as helpful as it once was.

One can predict, therefore, that the popularity of this scheme is likely to decline markedly owing to the April 2017 changes which are discussed below.

It is worth noting that this scheme can be based on cash accounting or invoice accounting (that is, applying the usual tax point rules), whichever the user prefers.

Since an outcome of the scheme is that input tax cannot be reclaimed, it will usually not serve the purposes of businesses whose margins are untypically low for the nature of business they are in. This might arise if their market strategy is to occupy the lowest price point in the market. Or they might be in a phase of significant investment in a business that will turn to profit at a later stage (though there are limited reliefs for those in that position, which should be considered carefully). By contrast, if it operates on higher margins than are common for the sector, the business is more likely to benefit financially from the scheme. Another factor to consider is that if the business outsources very much, the outsourcing costs may have VAT added, in which case the input tax forgone is likely to be higher than for others in that trade sector.

16.3 Qualification for joining

The scheme is open to VAT-registered entities (other than those in the exclusion list below), that predict as at the time of application that their taxable turnover will be £150k or less (excluding disposals of capital goods). That relates to a net of VAT figure. It does not refer to profit, nor does it refer to "profit cost". All supplies for VAT purposes are included, including some that might be referred to as "disbursements" (even though they are not disbursements in VAT terms). It does not, however, include exempt supplies. Suppliers relying on agent status to justify their low turnover must consider the issues discussed in **Chapter 6**, as they apply equally here.

The question is how one can predict compliance with this ceiling. The rule is that it is the expected turnover that is relevant, not the actual turnover, and this prevents the measure becoming retrospectively ineffective. However, if the turnover exceeds this limit from the outset, the business will need to demonstrate why the prediction was both valid and too pessimistic at the same time.

143

The flat rate scheme

If HMRC challenge the situation the taxpayer will need to disclose his reasons. It is advisable, therefore, to have a contemporaneous note of the reasons for the assumptions that are made. A note prepared at a later time (particularly after it is clear that the prediction was too cautious) runs the risk of HMRC challenging the premise that it reflects the views of the taxpayer at the time of applying for membership of the scheme (despite the possible argument that the taxpayer is able to recall his reasons accurately). If HMRC take the view that the basis is retrospectively contrived, the result could be disqualification from the scheme from the outset. The fact that HMRC admitted the business to the scheme upon the original application will have no bearing on this.

However, for those taxpayers whose original assumptions are valid, and for taxpayers where the original estimate is accurate but expansion occurs, there are different rules relating to the point at which they need to leave the scheme. This is best considered by reference to the terms for remaining in the scheme, and this leads automatically to a consideration of the terms for leaving it.

16.4 Qualification for remaining in the scheme

Confusingly, whereas the upper limit for joining the scheme is taxable turnover of £150,000 net of VAT, the threshold below which one must remain to continue in the scheme is £230,000 gross of VAT, comprising both taxable and exempt turnover. This is £191,667 on a net basis on an assumption that all supplies are at the 20% standard rate. However, of course, suppliers making exempt, zero or reduced rated supplies have more effective headroom.

This presumably reflects the fact that the business is operating on inclusive figures as its basic mode of accounting and can thus more easily monitor gross turnover. But that is not always the case, such as where B2B suppliers are invoicing on a net plus VAT basis. These run the risk of failing to appreciate that the upper limit is gross rather than net. It also reflects a quirk of the scheme as it relates to exempt supplies, which is discussed further below.

The sale of capital assets is ignored for this purpose.

The limit is considered in two ways, both being modelled on the VAT registration threshold.

One approach involves keeping a record of when the business started using the scheme (which, for many, will be the effective date of VAT registration). At the anniversary of that date, a check should be made to see whether the turnover exceeded the £230,000 threshold in the prior twelve months. If it did, the business must leave the scheme but, if it did not, it can (on that test) remain a member. However, if HMRC can be convinced that in the following twelve months the turnover will remain below £191,500 (on the gross basis), the business can remain in the scheme despite breaching the £230,000 in the prior year.

Another approach, independent of the above, is to consider, at any time, whether the business expects a turnover of £230,000 to arise within the next 30 days. If so, the entity leaves the scheme with effect from the beginning of the 30 days. Reference should be made to the discussion of that predictive test relating to registration for VAT, as discussed in **2.3.2**, for observations about such predictions. Whilst this second test may appear inherently unlikely to arise, consideration should be given to the possibility of exceptional exempt supplies triggering this condition (as well as the possible taxable supplies).

16.5 Other causes of either leaving the scheme or not qualifying for it *ab initio*

The following immediately make a business unqualified for the scheme:

- it makes supplies under the Tour Operators Margin Scheme;
- it uses a second hand margin scheme;
- it wishes to operate divisional registration;
- it forms a VAT group or is eligible to join one;
- it forms an intention to buy goods falling into the capital goods scheme;
- it is controlled by another party or another party controls it.

The last of these is an anti-avoidance provision which conspicuously reduces the potential usefulness of the scheme, effectively precluding its use in the case of corporate group operations. It is clear that the general purpose behind the provision is to offer help to simple "single-cell" businesses.

Voluntarily leaving the scheme

If the entity is entitled to remain in the scheme, but would prefer to leave, it can do this by writing to a prescribed office of HMRC. They normally remove the business from the scheme at the start of a new accounting period, but you are entitled to ask to leave in the middle of a period.

The entity is then precluded from re-joining the scheme for 12 months.

HMRC powers to direct departure from scheme

HMRC have overriding "protection of revenue" powers to withdraw the scheme from otherwise qualifying traders. There does not appear to be any significant record of HMRC deciding to do this, and it seems likely that the various automatic exclusions deal with most scenarios where they might have regarded their revenues as being under threat.

Changes in business activity

Where the business activity changes, for instance, such as to require a reclassification of the percentage, HMRC should be informed of this within 30 days. The business will need to consider applying a different percentage relating to the change in circumstances.

16.6 Issues arising from accounting under the scheme

These issues are discussed fully in Notice 733, but the following are points of interest that ought to be highlighted.

- The percentage applicable arises from the description of the main trade of the entity, or the closest possible description where there is not a perfect fit. This can lead to ambiguity as to which to select, which increases risk in operating the scheme. You are supposed to select the category. If you ask HMRC to opine on it, they will usually only indicate where they disagree and not put forward an alternative. This is an unhelpful aspect of what is supposed to be a simplification measure.

- That percentage applies to the sales figure on a gross of VAT (that is, VAT-inclusive) basis. The risk, here, is forgetting that and applying it only to the net figure, giving rise to a significant under-declaration.
- The percentage also applies to exempt turnover, which is extremely counter-intuitive. This means that any entity which has a side-line in, say, residential rents (which are exempt) is unlikely to want to join the scheme, as its liability will be too high relative to the underlying VAT liabilities of the activities. However, bank interest is ignored.
- You can operate either invoice or cash accounting under the scheme. Given that there are no inputs to claim (subject to the next point) the usual downsides of cash accounting do not apply, so it is quite attractive. However, for invoice based businesses, invoice accounting seems simpler.
- For those newly registered for VAT there is a reduction to the applicable rate (discussed below).
- There is limited ability to reclaim VAT even though the scheme is designed to eliminate input accounting. This reduces simplicity but is intended to decrease the impact of exceptional transactions. It allows capital goods purchases of more than £2,000 inclusive of VAT to be subject to VAT recovery (if, and to the extent that, that would be possible if accounting outside the scheme) as an offset against the output tax. There are conditions for this which are covered in Notice 733.

It can be seen from the above summary of the key issues that, despite this being a simplification scheme (which, in fairness, it succeeds in being) it is full of risks, and traps for the unwary. Counter-intuitive and seemingly unfair aspects abound, and can have disproportionate impacts.

16.7 Scheme percentages and the first-year discount

Those businesses which adopt the scheme straight after VAT registration will be interested in the discount applicable to the first year of VAT registration. It does not apply to the first year of using the scheme *per se*, but only to those newly VAT registered.

This allows the user to take away one percentage point from the applicable percentage. For instance, if the applicable percentage is 12.5%, the discounted percentage to apply is 11.5%. This welcome fiscal easement for the newly registered is clearly not a simplification. Indeed, it increases risk, because the requirement to move up to the full relevant rate after the first year might be missed.

16.8 Flat rate for low cost traders from April 2017

For many years the scheme was well understood to provide a mild fiscal boost to the small trader in most cases, particularly to those newly registered. Indeed, HMRC literature admitted as much.

However, apparent "industrial scale avoidance" was noted by HMRC where the users had very little input tax to forgo, and thus benefited from a flat rate taking into account a notional lost input tax deduction which was not realistic. HMRC decided to characterise this as "abuse" (despite the rules clearly allowing it as apparently an intended outcome) and therefore introduced an overriding higher flat rate for all traders in that category as defined. At the time of writing the percentage is 16.5%. As the rate of VAT is 20%, it is clear that the allowance for forgone input tax is virtually nil at this level (16.5% of a gross figure of £120 being broadly equivalent to 20% of the net £100). In other words, it works on the basis of simply imputing the highest possible tax yield from a stream income.

The rules for this "low cost trader" category are potentially complex and should be reviewed in Notice 733 and in the regulations. The following is a summary.

It will apply where the trader has very low purchases of goods (note – not services). Certain goods are not allowed to be deemed to be goods and are therefore not treated as creating a high level of goods purchases.

The rule applies where the qualifying goods purchases are worth less than 2% of the flat rate turnover, or less than £1,000 per year (pro-rated per period). If either of these value tests applies, the business defaults to the low cost trader percentage.

Goods which are not allowed for this test are:
- vehicle costs including fuel, unless operating in the transport sector using an owned or leased vehicle;

- food or drink for employees and owners;
- capital expenditure goods of any value;
- goods for resale, leasing, letting or hiring out if the main business activity does not ordinarily consist of selling, leasing, letting or hiring out such goods;
- goods that are to be re-sold or hired out, unless selling or hiring is the main business activity;
- goods for disposal, such as promotional items, gifts or donations.

Furthermore, the exclusion of all services is a singular aspect of the rule. The fact that many small traders may pay substantial taxable sums on royalties, subscriptions for technical resources, advertising and promotion, telecoms infrastructure and computing services, and so on, has been totally ignored in the introduction of this rule. It is prejudicial to the interests of all industries that rely heavily on services, which, after all, includes most of the smaller businesses.

At the risk of being rather dramatic, the changes of April 2017 have removed most of the point of the flat rate scheme.

16.9 Conclusion

The flat rate scheme is a good idea overall, but has become more complicated and risky than it ought to be, and is of little practical use to many. That said, advisers need to be aware of it to ensure that, where it can provide benefits, their clients can take advantage, subject to the caveat that care is needed in its application.

17. Policy issues relating to registration

To a great extent the question of economic or political policy surrounding the rules for VAT registration are irrelevant to the business which must comply with those rules, but a book of this nature provides a platform to air some thoughts on this subject.

The most noticeable aspect of the VAT registration rules is the fact that registration is not compulsory for all businesses. It is possible to run a taxable business and not register as long as the taxable turnover falls below a certain level. Why is this?

The politicians would like you to think that this is a business facilitation measure. The argument might be that micro-businesses suffer barriers to entry put up by larger and well established businesses and that allowing a business to start life with an in-built VAT advantage does no more than reduce the barrier to entry. In particular it might be said that the administrative burden for smaller businesses is a critical factor, and this is to some extent supported by the fact that businesses that do exceed the turnover limits are allowed to opt for more streamlined VAT administration up to a turnover of £150,000 (the flat rate scheme).

These ideas are so enticing that nobody questions them. But it is worth noting that few businesses that are above the threshold but can opt for the flat rate scheme do so unless they happen to save tax (though that is not the government's reason for its introduction) and this suggests that, irksome as "admin" is, it tends to be accepted in cases where money can be saved. Furthermore, B2B businesses often register voluntarily. So, is the saving in administrative effort really a major driver of the policy, and, if so, who is doing the saving?

A further point is that almost all other EU states apply much lower thresholds, yet we are never told that the reason for the sluggishness of the rest of the EU is their cripplingly low VAT registration threshold. Indeed, other parts, such as Germany and the Netherlands, are more vigorous, not less.

Perhaps the real reason is hinted at in article 281 of the *Principal VAT Directive*, which says:

> "Member States which might encounter difficulties in applying the normal VAT arrangements to small enterprises by reason of the activities or structure of such enterprises, may ... apply simplified procedures ... ."

It may well be the case that registering small enterprises for VAT is not cost effective for HMRC, so it is the administrative cost of government that is the target for reduction rather than the administrative costs of the business (though, of course, both are reduced). This is supported by the fact that the threshold is based on taxable turnover rather than on all turnover. Hence a large exempt sector business does not have to register for VAT until taxable supplies exceed the threshold, despite being perfectly large enough to be given no privileges on the basis of being small.

So, what problems can be seen to arise from a VAT registration threshold standing at around £85k?

- It is possible for a one man band or a two person partnership to earn a decent living if they incur only costs of their own labour without having to account for VAT.
- At the rate of 20%, the competitive advantage in avoiding the need to charge tax can be significant.
- In certain circumstances the extra turnover that needs to be generated in order to replace the money lost to VAT at that kind of threshold is around £11k-£12k, which is around 12%-13% (or perhaps two years' worth of average growth). This is a major disincentive to growth and to hiring employees to drive growth.
- There are certain sectors where unregistered tradesmen make life extremely difficult for the more established VAT registered businesses (assuming work which is standard rated), because the profit they can accept leaves their jobs at a price where the tax cost for the larger business leaves it making a loss.
- The degree of inequality arising from this gives rise to a ready temptation to indulge in business fragmentation or black market operation, thus favouring less scrupulous traders and in turn less scrupulous general trading practices.

151

- There is perhaps a general assumption that small businesses are VAT-free, thus increasing the risk that people will forget the potential liability to register at the correct time. If the threshold were lower, businesses would assume that they almost always needed to register, leaving less room for error. This would reduce the risk of catastrophic situations such as where a small unprofitable business fails to register on time and proceeds to trade unprofitably with ever increasing but unrecognised VAT liabilities.
- The public could not assume that a VAT registered business is necessarily "large", thus causing the public to fail to recognise the risk associated with dealing with a small business.

In general, the threshold has increased by more than inflation and the VAT rate has increased substantially in the same period. The "cliff edge" that has thus opened between unregistered and registered businesses has become extreme. The use of modern systems of control, based on overall risk, and capable of "detecting" problems in accounting records, should make sensible control of micro-businesses more streamlined for HMRC. It would significantly reduce the cost to collection ratio for such businesses. There would be a cut in resources spent on investigating businesses that are close to the threshold since almost no business would legitimately not be registered. The tax base would widen and thus create more room for general tax cuts. There would be greater confidence in business that everyone was bearing a fair share of the burden and thus less reporting of unfair trading to HMRC.

In a wide-ranging review of VAT compliance burdens in 2017, the Office of Tax Simplification drew attention to the high threshold and mentioned several of the points above. It stopped short of recommending a reduction, but floated that as a possibility. The Chancellor of the Exchequer immediately froze the threshold at the then £85k level, for two years, while a review of the registration threshold, and how it operated, could be carried out.

What can we expect from this?

If we assume that Brexit will give the government *carte blanche*, the following possibilities would be sensible.

The main issue identified by the OTS was the "cliff edge" of taxation when being registered at £85k. This could be tackled by giving allowances for traders which have lower turnovers above that level (say, up to £150k), only applicable on supplies to final consumers (so there is no relief where the buyer can claim the VAT). This could be by reference to a sliding scale of discounts applicable to the VAT on the sales (or the net payable figure) which would ratchet towards 100% the higher one's turnover goes towards the ceiling.

However, this would cost revenues to the government, and would be complicated to operate or to monitor. It would not address many of the other criticisms of the high threshold.

So, the logical solution would be to introduce a much lower threshold (say £30k), and apply graduated discounts, up to a turnover of, say £100k. Some revenue would be collected from those who are currently not taxed at all, so revenue yield would not be impacted. In due course, one might expect the discount to be reduced or discontinued following more general acceptance of the fact that VAT registration is at a lower turnover.

Perhaps VAT registration could become more automated and, at lower turnover levels, incorporated into the annual corporate tax return.

Consideration could be given to excluding some kinds of turnover from the thresholds, such as zero rated turnover (on which no tax would be charged). There could be a higher threshold for supplies of staff between corporate group members to reflect the fact that staff sharing is not a mainstream economic activity.

No doubt such ideas will be considered during the two year period, and, at risk of entering the risky world of predictive punditry, my guess would be a reduced registration threshold applying at some stage in the 2020s.

Law: EC/2006/112, art. 281

Appendix – Historic VAT registration thresholds

	£
April 2017 onwards	85,000
April 2016 – March 2017	83,000
April 2015 – March 2016	82,000
April 2014 – March 2015	81,000
April 2013 – March 2014	79,000
April 2012 – March 2013	77,000
April 2011 – March 2012	73,000

Table of primary legislation

Companies Act 2006
- 1159 .... 11.4.3
- Sch. 6 .... 11.4.3

Finance Act 2008
- 123 .... 14.5
- Sch. 41 .... 14.5

Limited Partnership Act 1907 .... 2.2, 11.4.4

Partnership Act 1890 .... 15.4

Value Added Tax Act 1994
- 3(1) 5.1
- 4 .... 5.1
- 8 .... 3.4
- 9A 11.6
- 43(1) 11.1
- 43B(5) 11.5
- 43B(6) 11.5
- 43B(7) 11.7
- 43C 11.9
- 46 .... Ch. 12
- 47 .... 6.3
- 49 .... 2.4.3
- 53 .... 6.4
- 77(4) 1.2.1
- 84(4C) 11.5
- Sch. 1 .... 2.3
- Sch. 1, para. 1 .... 2.3.1, 2.3.2, 2.4.3, 2.4.4, 2.4.7, 10.3
- Sch. 1, para. 2 .... 8.2.1
- Sch. 1, para. 9 .... 9.1
- Sch. 1, para. 11-13 .... 13.2.1
- Sch. 1, para. 14 .... 10.2
- Sch. 1A 2.3.4
- Sch. 1A, para. 1 .... 2.3.4
- Sch. 1A, para. 2 .... 2.4.6
- Sch. 1A, para. 2 .... 2.4.6
- Sch. 1A, para. 4 .... 2.3.4
- Sch. 1A, para. 13 .... 10.2

Sch. 2	2.5.2
Sch. 2, para. 1	2.5.2
Sch. 2, para. 2	2.5.2
Sch. 2, para. 3	2.5.2
Sch. 2, para. 4	9.7
Sch. 2, para. 6-7	13.2.3
Sch. 2, para. 10	2.5.2
Sch. 3, para. 1	2.5.1
Sch. 3, para. 5-7	13.2.2
Sch. 3A, para. 6	13.2.4
Sch. 3A, para. 9	2.5.3
Sch. 3B	2.5.4
Sch. 3B, para. 2	2.5.4
Sch. 4A	3.4
Sch. 6, Part 2	3.6
Sch. 6, para. 9	4.9
Sch. 9, Group 16	4.2
Sch. 9A	11.6
Sch. 10	3.5, 9.2
Sch. 33, para. 4	9.6

Table of secondary legislation

Statutory instruments

1987/1806 .... 6.4
1989/472 .... 3.5.2
1995/2518, reg. 94B 4.6, 4.7
2004/1931 .... 11.4.4

Council directive EC 2006/112 (The Principal VAT Directive)

.... 2.3, 4.2, 9.1, 9.4
art. 9 .... 5.1
art. 281 .... Ch. 17

Index of cases

A1 Lofts [2010] UKFTT 581 (TC) 6.2.1, 6.2.4
Apple and Pear Development Council v C & E Commrs C-102/86,
  [1988] STC 221..5.2.1
Belcher v HMRC [2017] UKFTT 427 (TC) 8.3
Belgium v Ghent Coal Terminal NV C-37/95 [1998] STC 260 .... 9.4
Beteiligungsgesellschaft Larentia and Minerva mbH & Co. KG
  v Finanzamt Nordenham C□108/14...11.3, 11.4.1
Brabners LLP v HMRC [2017] UKFTT 666 TC 4.8
C&E Commrs v Cantor Fitzgerald International C-108/99 [2011] 4.3
C&E Commrs v Lord Fisher [1981] STC 238 .... 5.2.2
C&E Commrs v Tilling Management Services [1979] STC 365.................. 4.4
C&E Commrs v Tron Theatre Ltd [1994] STC 177................................ 5.2.3
CEC v Republic of Finland C-246/08.. 5.2.3
De Ferranti v HMRC [2011] UKFTT 435 (TC) 5.2.2
Dennis Townsend and Maureen Townsend (VTD 17081).................. 8.3, 8.4
Fivegrange Ltd (VTD 5338) 7.2
Gravel Road Records Ltd v HMRC [2017] UKFTT 80 (TC) 5.2.2
Groundworks Cheshire [2012] UKFTT 750 (TC) 5.2.3
Intercommunale voor Zeewaterontzilting (INZO) v Belgian
  State C-110/94, [1996] STC 569.. 9.4
Keith Edward Jenkinson v C&E Commrs [1988] VATTR 45 .... 14.5
Keydon Estates Ltd (VTD 4471) 7.2
Latchmere Properties Ltd EWHC 133; Ch D [2005] STC 731 .... 7.2
Longridge on the Thames [2016] EWCA Civ 930.......................... 5.2.2, 5.2.3
Mark Reid (Reid & Co) [2013] UKFTT 241 TC..................................... 4.7
MG & ND Storer v HMRC [2017] UKFTT 776 (TC)................................ 3.2
Pentex Oil Ltd EDN/91/140 .... 4.7
Republic of Finland (2009) C-246/08... 5.2.2
Schmelz v Finanzamt Waldviertel C-97/09, [2011] STC 88.................. 2.3.4
Secret Hotels 2 [2014] UKSC 16... 6.2.1, 6.2.3
Spearmint Rhino Ventures (UK) Ltd v R&C Commrs [2007]
  EWHC 613, [2007] STC 1252...6.2.1, 6.2.2, 8.2.2
Strathearn Gordon Associates Ltd (VTD 1884) 7.2
Susan Evans v HMRC [2011] UKFTT 464 (TC).................................... 1.2.2
Three H Aircraft Hire v C&E Commrs [1982] STC 653 .... 9.1
Tolsma v Inspecteur der Omzetbelasting Leeuwarden
  C-16/93, [1994] STC 509.. 5.2.1
Trinity Mirror plc (formerly Mirror Group Newspapers
  Ltd) v C&E Commrs C-409/96.. 4.3
Yarburgh Children's Trust v C&E Commrs [2002] EWHC 2201............... 5.2.3

General index

13th directive regime
    de-registration 13.2.4
    registration requirement 2.5.3
Acquisition threshold
    goods from EU 2.5.1
Agent or principal
    blind agency 6.3
    case law 6.2
    implications 6.1
    practical considerations 6.2.5
    Tour Operators Margin Scheme 6.4
    Uber (EAT decision) 6.2.2
Barter
    constituting a supply 3.2
    interaction with reverse charge 3.4
Brexit
    registration policy issues .... Ch. 17
    UK as "third country" re MOSS 2.5.4
Broadcasting services
    non-established persons 2.3.4
    special VAT regime 2.5.4
Business
    changes in activity (flat rate scheme) 16.5
    charities and non-business activities 5.2.3
    economic activity (distinguished) 5.1
    fragmentation .... Ch. 8
    gifts (distinguished) 5.2.1
    hallmarks of 5.2.2
    hobby business 5.2.2
    joint activity 7.1
    meaning of 5.2
    private activities (distinguished) 5.2.2
    profit motive not relevant 5.2.2
    splitting .... Ch. 8
Capital assets
    look back test 2.3.1
    transfer of going concern 2.4.7
Charities
    business activities 5.2.3
    grants and donations 5.2.3

    group registration 11.3
    predominant concern test 5.2.3
    self supplies 3.5.3
Companies
    as registration entity 2.2
Compensation
    whether a supply 4.3
Compulsory registration
    criteria 2.1
    entities 2.2
Consideration
    profit (distinguished) 7.1
    third parties 2.3
Construction
    self supplies 3.5.2
De-registration
    compulsory 13.3
    disadvantages 13.2.3
    distance selling 13.2.3
    generally .... Ch. 13
    turnover test 10.3
    voluntary 13.2
Disbursements
    meaning and tax effect 4.8
Distance selling
    compulsory registration 2.5.2
    de-registration 13.2.3
    voluntary registration 9.7
Divisional registration
    principle and practicalities .... Ch. 12
Economic activity
    business (distinguished) 5.1
Electronic services
    Mini One Stop Shop 2.5.4
    non-established persons 2.3.4
    registration structure 2.5.4
Employee costs
    supplies 4.2
Entertainment and broadcast services
    special VAT regime 2.5.4
European Union
    acquisition of goods from 2.5.1, 9.6, 13.2.2
    distance selling liability 2.5.2
    registration for electronic services 2.5.4

voluntary de-registration 13.2.2
  voluntary registration 9.6
Face value vouchers
  whether a supply 3.3
Flat rate schemes
  accounting under the scheme 16.6
  causes of having to leave 16.5
  conditions for joining 16.3
  conditions for remaining in scheme 16.4
  first-year discount 16.7
  generally .... Ch. 16
  leaving the scheme 16.5
  low cost traders 16.8
  purpose of scheme 16.2
  scheme percentages 16.7
Foreign currency
  look back test 2.3.1
Form completion
  generally .... Ch. 15
  groups 15.5
  information to provide with application 15.3
  Isle of Man registration 15.6
  list of forms 15.2
  partnerships 15.4
  transfer of old VAT number 15.7
Fragmentation of business
  directions to treat as single entity 8.2
  HMRC defences 8.1
  impact of direction 8.2.3
  links (financial, economic, organisational) 8.2.2
  retrospective directions 8.3
Franchises
  business fragmentation issues 8.2.2
Grants and donations
  whether consideration for supply 5.2.3
Group registration
  anti-avoidance 11.4.4, 11.6
  application form 15.5
  control criteria 11.4
  entity criteria 11.3
  exceptional circumstances 11.7
  group membership 11.2
  HMRC refusal 11.5
  joint and several liability 11.1

   leaving a group 11.9
   meaning of control 11.4.3
   non-corporates 11.3
   partnership control 11.4.2
   phantom groups 11.8
   purpose 11.1
   timing of application 11.7
Hairdressers
   business fragmentation issues 8.2.2
Historic supplies test   see *Look back test*
Hobby business
   VAT registration 5.2.2
Hotels
   longer term occupants 4.9
Illegal activity
   whether within scope of VAT 5.3
Imported services
   as taxable supplies 3.4
Inherited turnover rule
   transfer of going concern 2.4.3
Install and assemble contracts
   non-established persons 2.3.4
Interest on rent
   as compensation.. 4.3
International activity
   grounds for registration 2.5
Isle of Man
   registration 15.6
Land and buildings
   look back test... 2.3.1
   non-established persons 2.3.4
   voluntary registration... 9.2
Land development
   profit or consideration 7.2
   voluntary registration... 9.2
Lease payments
   as compensation.. 4.3
   transfer of going concern 2.4.6
Limited partnerships
   as registration entity 2.2
Look back test
   acquisition of goods from EU 2.5.1
   distance selling liability 2.5.2
   foreign currency 2.3.1

generally	2.3.1
non-established persons	2.3.4
notification procedure	2.3.1
waiver of registration	10.3

Look forward test
acquisition of goods from EU	2.5.1
distance selling liability (no test for)	2.5.2
generally	2.3.2
interpreting the test	2.3.2
non-established persons	2.3.4
registration requirement	2.3.2
transfer of going concern	2.4.4

Management services
phoney services	4.5
taxable supplies	4.4

Mini One Stop Shop
distance selling	2.5.2
electronic services	2.5.4

Non-established persons
definition	2.3.4
mandatory registration	2.3.4

Non-UK established business
transfer of going concern	2.4.6

Office of Tax Simplification
review of compliance burdens	Ch. 17

Partnerships
application form	15.4
as registration entity	2.2
existence of	8.3
land development	7.2

Penalties
dishonest error	14.3
generally	Ch. 14
honest error	14.2
periods before April 2010	14.4
reasonable excuse	14.2

Place of supply rules
non-established persons	1.4, 2.3.4

Predicted taxable supplies test   see *Look forward test*

Predominant concern
charities	5.2.3

Principal or agent   see *Agent or principal*

167

Profit
  consideration (distinguished) 7.1
  land development 7.2
Reasonable excuse
  case law 14.5
  failure to register 14.2
Registration
  agent or principal .... Ch. 6
  business (existence of) .... Ch. 5
  business splitting .... Ch. 8
  commercial advantages 1.4
  compulsory registration criteria 2.1
  disadvantage 1.5
  distance selling 2.5.2
  divisional .... Ch. 12
  electronic services 2.5.4
  fiscal advantages 1.3
  flat rate scheme (registration for) .... Ch. 16
  groups of companies .... Ch. 11
  international activity 2.5
  penalties .... Ch. 14
  policy issues .... Ch. 17
  pros and cons .... Ch. 1
  risk mitigation 1.2
  taxable supplies 2.3, 3
  transfers of going concerns 2.4
  VAT-claimed goods 2.5.3
  voluntary .... Ch. 9
  waiver of requirement to register .... Ch. 10
Related companies
  delayed consideration 4.6
Residential providers
  self supplies 3.5.3
Reverse charge
  imported services 3.4
  non-established persons 2.3.4
Risk mitigation
  registration 1.2
Security payments
  HMRC power to demand 14.6
Self supplies
  charities 3.5.3
  construction 3.5.2

    registration requirement 3.5
    residential providers 3.5.3
Software supply services
    special VAT regime 2.5.4
Sole proprietors
    as registration entity 2.2
Solicitors
    disbursements 4.8
Supplies
    barter 3.2
    compensation 4.3
    definition .... Ch. 3
    disbursements 4.8
    face value vouchers 3.3
    grants and donations 5.2.3
    illegal activity 5.3
    imported services 3.4
    management services 4.4
    self supplies 3.5
    staff 4.2
    subsidies 5.2.3
    valuation 3.6
Supply and fit contracts
    non-established persons 2.3.4
Taxable supplies
    criteria for registration 2.3
Taxis
    business fragmentation issues 8.2.2
Telephone services
    non-established persons 2.3.4
Time limits
    for HMRC assessments 1.2.1
Time of supply
    delivery 2.3.3
Tour Operators Margin Scheme
    special VAT treatment 6.4
    VAT groups 11.3
Transfer of going concern
    definition 2.4.7
    from unregistered transferor 2.4.5
    generally 2.4
    inherited turnover rule 2.4.3
    look forward test 2.4.4
    no purchase price 2.4.2

    non-UK established business 2.4.6
    registration requirements 2.4.1
    VAT number (transfer of) 2.4.8
Transfer of old VAT number
    form completion 15.7
    transfer as going concern 2.4.8
Transport-related services
    non-established persons 2.3.4
UK stock holding
    non-established persons 2.3.4
Unincorporated bodies
    group registration... 11.3
Unregistered transferor
    transfer of going concern 2.4.5
VAT-claimed goods
    registration requirement.. 2.5.3
VAT number
    transfer as going concern 2.4.8
Voluntary registration
    acquisitions from other EU states 9.6
    business (requirement to have).. 5.2.2
    distance selling 9.7
    intention to trade 9.3
    land and property 9.2
    nature of taxable supplies 9.5
    reasons to register.. 9.1
    speculative ventures.. 9.4
Waiver of registration requirement
    overview 10.1
    predicted turnover... 10.3
    zero-rated supplies 10.2
Website supply
    special VAT regime... 2.5.4
Zero-rated supplies
    waiver of registration requirement... 10.2

Printed and bound in Great Britain by
Marston Book Services Limited, Oxfordshire